Chickens
Eat Pasta

Clare Pedrick

Chickens Eat Pasta

ESCAPE TO UMBRIA

Matador
9 Priory Business Park,
Wistow Road, Kibworth Beauchamp,
Leicestershire. LE8 0RX
Tel: (+44) 116 279 2299
Fax: (+44) 116 279 2277
Email: books@troubador.co.uk
Web: www.troubador.co.uk/matador

ISBN 978-1784623-517

British Library Cataloguing in Publication Data.
A catalogue record for this book is available from the British Library.

Printed and bound by CPI Group (UK) Ltd, Croydon, CR0 4YY
Typeset in 11pt Aldine by Troubador Publishing Ltd, Leicester, UK

Matador is an imprint of Troubador Publishing Ltd

MIX
Paper from
responsible sources
FSC
www.fsc.org   FSC® C013604

To Max, Juliana and Georgie
This is where it all began

The Author

Clare Pedrick is a British journalist. She studied Italian at Cambridge University before becoming a reporter. This book describes how, as a young woman, she bought an old ruin in Umbria. She went on to work as Rome correspondent for the Washington Post and as European Editor of an international features agency. She still lives in Italy with her husband, whom she met in the village where she bought her house. The couple have three children.

Prologue

People often ask me what made me do what I did. I reply that life is not always a case of making conscious choices. If I have learned one thing, it is that following your instincts often leads to happiness, even if it doesn't mean taking the easiest path you could have chosen.

Chapter One

The dripping was becoming louder, settling into a relentless rhythm. It had started as a barely audible whisper in the treetops outside the kitchen window, flung open to let the newly washed floor dry. The drops fell more heavily now, thudding overhead on the terracotta roof tiles. A small puddle had formed quickly on the dark red floor, spreading from one rectangle to another as the wind drove the rain in through the open space. The window banged shut abruptly and blew open again violently as the summer storm ripped through the mountains. I let go of my grip on the mop to secure the fragile window frame with its ancient wooden latch. Now I'd have to start all over again. There wasn't much time. Angela and Ercolino would be here soon to drive me to the station.

Suddenly, the tears that had been welling up deep inside me all morning brimmed over and began coursing down my cheeks. I crouched down on the still wet floor. How could it all have gone so wrong?

It was strange really, how rain could make such a difference. Outside, a thick white mist was rising rapidly, shrouding the tree-lined mountain and swiftly wiping out the almost cloudless sky that had cast shafts of light through the window just a few minutes earlier. Of course, it had been raining that day this whole business had started. That was fairly normal for November in England, but this time it had poured ceaselessly, for days on end, casting me further and further into a trough of despair and loneliness.

Until I saw the advertisement, as I thumbed through the soggy pages of the hefty newspaper that I had bought to while away yet another miserable

Sunday morning on my own. That had changed everything. Or so it had seemed. But then, maybe I had been asking for trouble. There were plenty of people who were sure it could only end badly. As my sensible aunt Vi had said when I told her what I'd done.

"How can you buy a house just because you've watched a video?"

★★★

The chicken was teasing out something long and slippery in its beak. It swallowed it in a few short movements and bent its scrawny neck to peck up another strand from a small pile on the ground. Nearby, an old woman with a stooping gait watched for a few minutes before moving off to empty her plastic bucket in front of several other chickens emerging from the lower part of an old stone house. She murmured something barely audible as she bent down to poke a bony finger at the thighs of the two larger birds. The sound quality of the video was poor and the image flickered and jolted every now and then.

"She's checking to see which one to have for Sunday lunch," whispered the Englishman, moving closer to the television screen where the video was playing.

"That's spaghetti she's giving them. Chickens eat pasta in this part of Italy."

The camera zoomed in on the plumpest chicken pecking at what would be its last meal, and a very small cup of coffee appeared on the side table next to me.

"Have an espresso," said my host, busying himself to make some space. "I bought the machine the last time I was over there. The secret is in packing the coffee really tight before you put it to heat, but I think I've got the hang of it now." He turned to move a pile of papers off a chair so that he too could take a seat.

"Sorry about the mess by the way, but you caught me a bit off guard."

Tearing my eyes away from the screen for a moment, where

shaky images of cobbled streets and pretty stone arches continued to float by, I surveyed what must be the sitting room of the small terraced house in Hove where I had rung the bell half an hour earlier. The walk from my own house had taken less than ten minutes, through the rain-soaked streets of Brighton, as it struggled to come to life on a dismal autumn morning. It was a Monday, and instead of heading to the offices of the newspaper where I was a reporter, I had turned my steps in the direction of the address that I had underlined heavily in red felt tip when I had first read the advert in the Sunday paper the day before.

"House for sale in hidden Umbria. Steve Parr & Associates."

Turning first to the overseas property section had long been a habit as I went through the weekend section of the national papers, but this time was different. The address on the advert was just a few streets away. Maybe it was a sign? In any case, I had more time on my hands than I knew what to do with right now, and no real ties here anymore.

It had been my turn to work the Saturday night shift at the newspaper, so Monday was a free day. That was the rule in the newsroom, a way of compensating journalists for long Saturday evenings that invariably involved covering drunken brawls between skinheads and rockers.

It wasn't clear who his associates were, but Steve Parr showed no sign of being fazed by the unannounced visit as he led the way into the room he had rigged up as his office. On the wall was a framed relief map of central Italy, with a range of jagged points in one corner, giving way to gentler slopes and a few spots of blue which must be lakes.

"I've only really just started this business," he said with an apologetic air, searching under a pile of magazines for the video cassette. "It's such a spectacularly beautiful place, so close to Rome in some ways, and yet so very different and completely unspoilt. It's like turning back the clock at least fifty years."

Three cups of espresso later, I emerged into the sodden street. Trying to dodge the puddles, I crossed the road and headed along the seafront towards home. The waves were crashing violently against the pebble beach. That was bound to be the front page for this evening's edition: *Storms Batter Sussex Coast!* It was the autumn version of that other headline that came round with the first few rays of sunshine every summer: *Sussex Sizzles into the Seventies!*

The summer seemed such a long time ago now, and all the misery it had brought with it. The rows, the break-up, the last minute cancellation of the holiday in Greece. Here I was, 26-years-old, alone and numb with boredom at the prospect of a future which until recently had seemed to be just what I wanted. At least there would be no problem getting time off. The news editor could hardly complain if I took a few days' leave after working for months without a break.

The next step would be to book a flight, and armed with some numbers of bucket shops in London, handed to me by Steve Parr as he showed me to the door, I pulled off my dripping coat and ran down the stairs into the basement kitchen of my house to get the phone. I glanced out of the rain-spattered window, trying not to notice the long green streak of mildew which was working its way down the whitewashed outside wall that led up to the small rear garden. It was impossible to miss the damp stains that were creeping up the walls inside the kitchen. The pretty little Regency house that had seemed so captivating when Rob and I had first looked round it three years ago was beginning to show signs of neglect. A loud telephone ring interrupted my thoughts. Damn. Who could that be?

"Oh there you are at last. I've been trying to get hold of you all morning." It was Vi, my maiden aunt. She was a matron at a hospital in Somerset and took her role very seriously as the last remaining senior member of the family, though tact was never her strong point. Nor was brevity for that matter. I braced myself.

"I wanted to tell you that I'm thinking of you on this very sad day. Can you hear me?" she boomed. I held the receiver a bit further away from my ear. Vi's family nickname was Foghorn.

"It doesn't seem possible that your father died a year ago today. And so soon after your poor mother." She paused to draw breath. "It must be especially hard now that you don't have a man any more. We all thought you'd be all right when you two were together. But now I worry about you. Your brothers are worried about you too. You're young and pretty, I'm sure you'll find someone else."

It was another five minutes before she hung up, making me promise that I would eat properly and ring her if I needed anything. Somehow, there hadn't been time to tell her that I was on my way to Italy, perhaps to buy a house in a village where chicken ate spaghetti.

The best way was to get a train from Rome, said Steve – we were on first name terms now and had spoken several times by phone since that first meeting. I should stay in a town called Terni, where his Italian business partner would pick me up from my hotel on Thursday morning. It had taken less than twenty four hours to make up my mind, and book a flight, leaving on Wednesday.

The next day and a half passed in a whirlwind, as I ventured out in the still sheeting rain to get some Italian lire from the bank. The teller passed me a thick wad of well worn notes in exchange for my small pile of crisp ones, the total amounting to a sum with a bewildering array of noughts. I stopped at a bookshop to buy a map of Italy and a bottle of Chianti from the delicatessen. Later that evening, glass in hand, it occurred to me that although I had a degree in Italian from one of Britain's best universities, I didn't have a clear idea of where Umbria was.

The hours dragged slowly next day. I was covering the inquest of a middle-aged man who had fallen to his death below Beachy Head further along the Sussex coast several weeks earlier. A police officer gave evidence from the family that the man had been a keen bird watcher.

"So it is possible," said the coroner, without much conviction in his voice, "that the deceased lost his footing while pursuing an unusual bird to get a closer look, and tragically slipped and fell over the cliff. The court returns an open verdict and our condolences go to his wife and two children."

At least they would get some money from the life insurance. I hastily wrote up the story and phoned it over to the newsdesk, mentally making a checklist of what I should pack as I spelt out the name of the dead man to the copytaker, a garrulous woman called Sylvia, who had bleached blonde hair and took a keen interest in the personal lives of all the journalists. The copytakers' room was right next to the newsroom, and when Sylvia wasn't taking down stories over her headphones, she would sit chatting to her colleagues about the reporters on the other side of the glass.

"I hear you're off to Italy dear," she said as I signed off my inquest piece. "Do you good, if you ask me. You've been looking really peaky lately, if you don't mind me saying. I suppose you're missing your boyfriend."

Less than twenty four hours later, after a flight sitting next to a friendly young Italian couple, the rail journey from Rome to Terni gave a taste of what was in store. The train rattled along and the wide open spaces turned into rolling hills and dramatic valleys, dotted with pale-coloured stone villages and olive groves that tumbled down the slopes.

"*Birra, aranciata, coca-cola, panini,*" chanted a gawky looking teenage boy. He lugged a plastic bucket full of cans up and down the corridor. Everyone in the carriage seemed intent on eating or drinking something, and the boy was doing a brisk trade. A few seats away from me, a couple of smartly dressed businessmen were earnestly engaged in a discussion that appeared to revolve around recipes for risotto.

"The trick is to keep stirring it all the while. I read my sales reports while I'm doing it," said the older of the two, leaning forward over his leather briefcase.

"You should try adding a small lump of butter at the end, just before you serve it. It makes all the flavours blend together," said the other, standing up and smoothing down a smart tobacco coloured linen suit. "I think we must be here."

The sound of brakes and a loud hissing interrupted the eavesdropping session, and a man in a neat blue uniform appeared on the platform, hurriedly donning a peaked red cap and waving a red flag.

"*Terni, stazione di Terni,*" boomed a crackly voice over the tannoy.

Terni was certainly not the prettiest place. The first glimpse on emerging from the station showed it to be disappointingly modern, the forecourt dominated by a large geometric steel sculpture. Several wide avenues branched out from the piazza, filled with people walking purposefully, or cycling in and out of the busy traffic.

"*Taxi Signorina?*"

"*Er, no grazie. Il mio albergo e' qui vicino,*" I said haltingly. It was the longest sentence I had uttered since setting foot in Italy and it was reassuring to see how effortlessly it tripped off the tongue. Carla would be proud of me. It was partly down to her that I was here at all, and she had often been in my thoughts over the past few days, a vision in her glamorous clothes, with the intoxicating perfume she always wore and that fascinating gold watch which was part of a bracelet and which she played with constantly as she waved her hands around. Carla was the wonderfully exotic creature who had first introduced me to Italian when I was still a 16-year-old schoolgirl. In our rather drab convent school, where the nuns wore floor-length black habits and a perpetual scowl on their faces, this flamboyant Italian teacher had been like a breath of fresh air. Her greatest wish, as she told our small sixth-form class almost every lesson, was that we would go and live in Italy and marry an Italian.

"Italian men make such wonderful husbands," she would whisper, breaking off from the Pirandello play she had been reading out loud. There was a touch of regret in her voice. For as all the girls knew, Carla had married an Englishman.

"Well I might manage the first request, but I'm afraid definitely not the second one Carla," I muttered to myself. I picked up my bag and walked towards the curiously named Hotel de Paris, whose sign was visible further up the longest avenue.

The hotel looked as if it might have been built in the 1950s, possibly in rather a hurry, with a flat façade and surly grey paint. Inside, the theme was a faint orange colour, with wooden furniture. There was no restaurant service, except for breakfast, I was told. The receptionist handed me a heavy key attached to a red silk sash. But there was a very good *trattoria* just around the corner in Piazza Tacito.

The agent who came to collect me from my hotel the next morning was a large well-coiffed lady called Mirella. She had a gravelly voice, the result, it seemed likely, of the number of cigarettes she clearly smoked. She had an unlit one in her hand, using it as a prop as she outlined the day's programme. My guide did her best to speak to me in English, though you could tell it didn't come easily.

"If you will rejoin the car er, it will be possible for me to accompany you to check the er, establishments in which you are, er, interested," she said, leading me outside. I reassured her that I spoke Italian. A look of relief mixed with disappointment registered on her face. She had clearly been practising for this moment. Mirella pointed towards a white Fiat Uno and opened the passenger door to remove what looked like a pile of children's' dirty football kit on the seat. She threw it into the back.

"*Prego!*" said Mirella. The car moved forward, into the busy stream of traffic.

"Do you care if I smoke?" She reached over onto the dashboard to find a lighter, encased in an embossed leather holder.

We were on our way to a place called Narni, Mirella explained. It was famous for the *Corsa all'Anello*. Had I heard of it? She turned towards me as she asked the question, taking her eyes off the road. We had left the traffic behind and were heading out into the countryside, with narrow winding lanes.

"No, I'm afraid not," I said. Unlike the driver, my gaze was fixed steadily on the sharp bends ahead. Mirella fumbled in her bag for something.

"Here, take this. It will explain everything. It is a race for horses."

The photographs on the brochure she handed me showed a procession in medieval dress, with what looked like nobles and their wives bedecked in long velvet robes promenading through cobbled streets. Another picture showed a man in a doublet astride a chestnut horse, deftly aiming a long spear at a tiny metal ring suspended at shoulder height. All around him, people in normal clothes appeared to be clapping and cheering.

"Yes, it is so fun. You must go. Look, we are arrived. Here is the house I want to show you."

The property Mirella had in mind was down a narrow alleyway in a gracious little town with towers and winding streets that opened out into a piazza, filled with cafes and *trattorias*. I liked the feel of the place immediately. The house was a tall slender construction with thick stone walls and tiny windows. It was almost ready to move into and very charming in a picture postcard kind of way.

"All you need is to buy some sh…, er er, the covers for the bed, and you could sleep there right away," said Mirella. "I always have trouble with that one," she said, reddening slightly. "My English teacher says I make it sound a rude word."

By now we had repaired to a nearby bar for lunch, where customers were already lined two deep, eating slices of pizza at the counter. Mirella pointed to what looked like half a British Rail sandwich sitting on a plate in the display unit and ordered two for each of us, filled with tomato and mozzarella.

"What would you like to drink?"

I asked for a glass of white wine.

"*Un vino bianco e un Crodino,*"

Next to the glass of wine the barman poured for me, he placed a squat bottle of fizzy amber liquid. He tipped it into a tumbler. Mirella saw the expression on my face.

"You don't have *Crodino* in England? Ah yes, you have beer. My teacher tells me. But I am habstemious."

She paused to attract the barman's attention again, and order another two sandwiches, this time with tuna and artichokes. They were actually much better than they looked. We had coffee – time for another cigarette – and Mirella called the barman again and listed what we had eaten. He rapidly did a calculation and announced that we owed eight thousand lire. It sounded a fortune, but in fact it was less than the price of a beer and a sandwich back home. I moved to pay, but in spite of her bulk, Mirella proved extremely agile and slapped down a ten thousand lire note. "No, today you are my guest." She asked the barman for a *gettone*, which I saw was a strange double-grooved coin that she fed into the public phone in the corner of the bar.

"I must call Cesare. He is my husband and I will tell him I will be late," she said. "I can see you like the house in Narni. But before you, er, make the final act, I must, er accompany you so you can rejoin another dwelling."

The place Mirella wanted to show me was in need of some repair, she said, but it had something rather special about it. Driving along the winding roads which seemed to stretch forever, she chatted about some of the people who lived in the village, breaking into Italian when her patience ran out with her English. It was a struggle to follow what she was saying in either language, with the views of the countryside vying for my attention and often winning the battle. Blue-hazed hills rolled in every direction, with a few small stone villages clutching onto the sides at impossible angles.

Mirella drove around the last bend on a small road that seemed to lead nowhere, and revved her Fiat Uno up a steep sloping drive. I gasped. Suddenly, I saw exactly what she meant by special. The house – or what was left of it – towered imposingly from its position on a knoll overlooking an endless vista of hills and valleys. It was built of a warm yellow coloured stone that was gradually being bathed in pink in the glow of the late afternoon sun. If you craned your neck you could just make out the rooftops of the miniscule village of San Massano a short distance away. This was the oldest inhabited settlement in Umbria. Mirella led the way up the rest of the pot-holed drive. About half-way up, the Fiat had made it clear it would go no further.

"The village's history goes back at least to the 10th century, and probably a great deal further," said Mirella, who had long switched back into Italian. "As for the house, no one knows really. For generations, it belonged to the same family. But then there was some kind of a quarrel, and the house was divided into two parts." She paused to disentangle herself from the brambles which had wound themselves around one of her legs, making a rip in her dark blue tights.

"*Porco dio!*"

The house was indeed in need of repair, with gaping holes in the terracotta-tiled roof and the outside stone walls badly crumbling. In some places they had completely collapsed. Inside, some sections of the uneven floors were missing, with dizzying drops down to the space below.

"Careful where you put your feet," said Mirella. She tugged at my arm to stop me from wandering into a cavernous room with hardly any floor at all. A large rat darted out between us.

It was hard to say how many rooms there were, or how many there might one day be. The building was huge and rambling, but there were no bedrooms that could be identified as such and certainly no bathroom. There was nothing that looked remotely like a kitchen and there appeared to be no electricity. The only source of water was from a conical-shaped stone construction to one side of the main building. Leaning over to look down into the well, I could just make out the shape of a dead fox floating in the water, its body bloated but its brush still intact. Incredibly, one part of the property was still inhabited, by an old man who peered out of a small broken window as we passed by.

Half an hour later we were seated in a village bar with a spectacular view of a tiny, shimmering lake. I touched my glass of prosecco to Mirella's Crodino. "It's the most beautiful place I've ever seen. I'll take it!"

Even Mirella looked a little taken aback.

"Don't you want to talk it over, with your parents or someone?"

"No, it's just what I want, really. I think it's perfect."

When the news got out, it would be difficult to say who was the more surprised. My two brothers, who were the only close relatives I now had, did little to hide their concern about what they said was an almost certainly unwise decision.

"So what does your surveyor say about the place," asked Charles, the older of the two, when I excitedly told him over a crackly phone line about the beautiful old house I had bought in the Umbrian hills. I admitted that I had not consulted a surveyor. It hadn't crossed my mind.

"Well what about your lawyer?" pursued Charles sensibly. I had to confess that I had not sought any legal advice at all.

"Well, never mind. We're still in time to stop this going through," he said, in a tone that was meant to be reassuring. I told him that it was way too late. I had already paid for the house, writing out a cheque in Mirella's office the previous day. It wasn't any great sum, though it was for me, representing a sizeable chunk of the money that my parents had left me. The price I paid would not have been enough for a deposit on a flat back in Brighton.

As for the villagers, they could not begin to understand what a young woman was doing on her own, so far from home.

"Don't you have a mother or a father?" asked a small white-haired man when Mirella introduced me to him the following day. We had driven back to take another look at the property I had just bought, so that I could take some photographs. The man, who looked to be in his fifties, was wandering around the village piazza, about five hundred yards from my house. He wore a white buttoned overall, with a thick brown jumper showing underneath.

"What about a husband? You don't want to end up like me."

Mirella had already given me a run-down on Tito the village shopkeeper, and on several of the forty two people who lived in San Massano.

"Forty three counting you," she said.

"Tito never married, mainly because he spent much of his

life caring for his old parents," said Mirella, who seemed to know everything about everyone.

"One of his sisters emigrated to Australia. His mother is dead but his father is still alive and Tito takes great care of him. You'll see him shaving the old man on the balcony in the mornings."

Thin and gaunt, his pale skin pulled tightly over his cheekbones, Tito stretched out a hand to shake mine.

"I would like to be the first person to welcome you to San Massano," he said. "And I hope that you find a husband one day soon."

That was just about the last thing on my mind at present. All I could think about was the house that I had just bought, and what it would look like when it was restored. I was in no doubt whatsoever that somehow the renovation would be managed, though I had no clear idea how. I had a living to earn back in Brighton, winter was closing in on the Umbrian hills, and I knew absolutely nothing about the building trade. Nor did I have anyone to help me.

That evening, under the noisy shower back in the Hotel de Paris, I started to make plans. The money would go through from my account in a matter of a few days, so the property would soon be in my name. Mirella had said her husband Cesare could take care of the renovation work, and assured me it would not take long.

"He doesn't have so much work on now," she had said. "He has his own small building firm – or at least he had before his business partner walked off with all the profits from a skiing village they were working on up in the mountains."

If they started quickly, as Mirella said, most of the structural work could be done by Christmas. I'd have some more time off due to me by then, and could come out and stay for a week or so. Christmas was bound to be fun here, with everyone throwing their houses open. I should organise a house-warming party of my own. It would be a chance to meet all the people who were to be my neighbours. I'd need a new dress or two. Maybe there would be time to find something in Rome before I flew back in a couple of days' time? Or in Terni? The water in the shower was beginning to turn cold. Time to get a move on. I had been invited to dinner with Mirella and her husband and she'd be here any minute to pick me up.

Mirella's house, when we reached it, reminded me of a hairdresser with an unremarkable haircut. Although Mirella sold houses for a living, hers was quite unremarkable. It wasn't actually a house at all, but a three-bedroomed apartment in what looked like any other street in Terni.

"It's just down the road from the Church of San Valentino," said Mirella, pushing the button to call the lift. "You know, San Valentino. He was the bishop of Terni. Then he was martyred." Of course – otherwise he wouldn't have been a saint. My convent education had taught me that much.

"Japanese couples come to get married here on San Valentino's day, February 14th, every year," she went on. It must come as quite a shock when they actually turn up, I thought. I couldn't think of a less romantic place to get married.

Cesare opened the door while Mirella was still looking for the key in her bag. He was an enormous man with a small goatee beard and a smile that started in the crinkles around his eyes and worked its way down his huge face. Cesare was the leader of the local boy scouts group. He indicated a chair for me at the dinner table. Unlike some people, he said pointedly, he had a conscience, and he would take it upon himself to make sure that no one would cheat the *signorina inglese*.

"I am a scout, and just like your Baden Powell, I am a man of honour," said Cesare, pronouncing his hero's first name like the German spa town. Seated at the head of the dinner table, he opened a bottle of wine, sniffing the cork appreciatively. Cesare was flanked on one side by his wife who nodded, ready to translate if I should need it, and on another by a couple who were introduced as their very good friends. They also had a small house in San Massano where they often spent weekends.

"She's one of your lot," said the husband in rapid, though far from perfect English, with a strange twang of Liverpuddlian that became especially strong when he swore, which seemed to be quite often. This was Ercolino, whose name, he quickly told me, meant Little Hercules, though he had a problem deciding where to put his aitches, so he pronounced it Ercules. The name suited him rather well. He was a small man in his fifties with twinkling eyes and a cigarette in one hand, which he waved around constantly as he became more animated. He pointed to his wife, a red-haired woman a few years younger, who had been speaking Italian at high speed to Mirella.

"She's English you know, but she's not so English any more. She's been away too long," he said, laughing loudly, jabbing his cigarette in the direction of his spouse.

Angela, his wife, had indeed been away a long time. As more dishes appeared on the table, and Cesare poured the wine, the couple told how they had met and run off to get married nearly twenty years earlier. They interrupted each other as they remembered the details.

"Cesare and Ercolino went to school together as boys," said Angela, lighting a cigarette of her own. "It wasn't long after the war, in Terni."

"The war left such poverty, and it was all the fault of you bloody English," interjected Ercolino. "Your airplanes flattened Terni to wipe out the steelworks here which was making weapons for Mussolini. And the bloody Americans helped with the bombing."

Puzzled, I asked how the war had played a role in his meeting Angela all those years later.

"*Pazienza.* I'll get to that bit in a minute," he said.

The experience of being brought up in those harsh times left Ercolino with two convictions, he recalled. He paused to stretch out his plate for another helping of Mirella's home-made *tortellini.* The first was that he would never again eat courgettes, one of the few things his parents could grow in their tiny allotment to feed their family of eight children. The second was that he would always have nice shoes. For much of his childhood, Ercolino and his brothers and sisters had had to make do with strips of old tyres cut into the shape of soles by his mother and tied to the children's feet with lengths of twine from old hay bales.

"You can't believe how hard it was to run with those things on your feet," he said. He downed another glass of red wine and shook his head at the memory.

Ercolino had left Italy for England almost as soon as he left school, drawn by the idea of working in a country where he had heard that people had money and knew how to enjoy themselves. It was the early Sixties and the young Italian soon found work as a waiter after landing in Liverpool.

"There was music in the air," he said, switching constantly between broken English to Italian. "That's where I met Angela. It's funny that we fell for each other really. We were so different – like cheese and chalk."

Angela had come over to stay for the weekend from her home across the water in the Isle of Man, she explained, taking up the story again. She was the daughter of wealthy Jewish parents and her future had already been decided, including her marriage to the son of a respectable family who attended the same synagogue.

"He was a nice Jewish boy, but it would never have worked, though I would probably have been a lot richer," said Angela. Ercolino's parents were Catholics, but had very little money. His father stoked the fires in the steelworks and his mother stayed at home to look after a small vegetable plot and a few chickens in the backyard. Both were members of the Italian Communist Party.

In Liverpool, Angela was initially attracted by the young Italian waiter's winklepickers, which were made out of soft black leather and were unmistakably stylish.

"I fell for his shoes," she said. She laughed at the memory, running her fingers through her hair.

He was captivated by her rich auburn curls and the way she looked at him when she said his name. The pair realised that there was no future for them together in either of their home countries, so six weeks after their first meeting they slipped off and caught a boat to Sweden where they got married in a registry office.

"And that was bloody that," said Ercolino. He blew his wife a kiss.

A loud crash came from next door.

"*Santo cielo.*" Mirella stood up and rushed out of the room and her voice could be heard remonstrating with her two children.

"*Basta* Danni! Stop it Roberto!"

I had met them on my way in, two boys who looked to be about six and eight years old, both with tightly cropped hair. Their mother had indulgently rubbed their heads as they took a break from a game that appeared to consist of jumping off the kitchen table and climbing back on to do it again.

"*Bambini eh!*" said Cesare, with a look of resignation. "Here, try some of this. It's traditional at this time of year." He pushed over a ceramic dish containing something which looked like a misshapen pig's trotter. That was precisely what it was, I discovered, though thankfully it had been hollowed out and stuffed with a mixture of sautéed pieces of salame, meat and herbs. Around the side were rich dark-coloured lentils. "Have some. They are lucky for bringing money," said Cesare. "You'll need some of that, though don't worry, I'll make sure it's not too much."

Cesare kept his word and in the weeks that followed my return to England, he sent me regular updates on my house, "*il castello di Clare*", "Clare's castle", as he called it. Each letter was typed on a single sheet of paper, with a list of the purchases made so far and an explanation of the work carried out. I would often find myself gazing at the latest missive at my desk in the newsroom, my notes from the magistrates' court hearing that I had attended earlier that morning carelessly pushed to one side.

"Are you sure you're all right? You've never missed a deadline before, but you seem a bit distracted lately." Caroline, the usually brusque assistant news editor, peered over my shoulder with an expression of concern. I hurriedly shoved Cesare's latest progress report under some notebooks and pulled out the story that I should have handed in half an hour earlier. She was right, of course. My mind was no longer completely on the job.

She wasn't the only one to notice.

"You're in love aren't you? Tell me who it is. I bet he's Italian."

Patrick was my closest friend at the newspaper. He lived next door but one and we'd often go for a drink together at the Eagle on the way home, to moan about a particularly harrowing day in the newsroom, or to berate the latest absurd story we'd been asked to cover. He had let me cry on his shoulder more than once in the months since my break up with Rob, and I in turn had offered whisky and sympathy during the final phases of his long and tortured relationship with a girl who lived in London.

"So go on, what's his name?"

"I don't know what you mean."

"You've been staring into space all morning, and you hardly touched your food in the canteen at lunchtime. And you keep looking at some kind of photograph, though I can't see who it is. If you ask me, your behaviour is decidedly shifty."

"*Buongiorno!*" Jed, the arts reporter, passed by my desk seconds after Patrick had left. "I brought you a cappuccino." He placed a frothy concoction in a plastic cup in front of me. "I know you only drink Italian coffee these days."

Sipping the milky brew as Jed moved off to write his theatre review, I pulled out Cesare's letter again. He had found a local builder in nearby Spoleto, a man from his parish church who was, he said, scrupulously honest. Between them, they had set about finding ways to save me money. The bath was second-hand but never used, since it had come from one of the unfinished apartments in the skiing village that was now abandoned. Cesare had got a scouting contact who was also an electrician to do the wiring. The flooring was finished, the roof mended and the house was beginning to take shape. He suggested that I get Benedetto, a handyman who lived in the village, to put up shelves and do other odd jobs when I next came over, and he told me that Angela and Ercolino had been looking after the accounts, paying my electricity bills for me with some money I had left them. After our meeting over dinner, Angela and Ercolino had insisted on helping me.

"I'm not sure you really know what you've taken on," said Angela, as we sat in a bar having coffee together the day after the dinner at Mirella's. We were in Terni, and in less than hour my train would leave for Rome where I would be catching my flight home.

"It's not easy finding your way around in Italy, and I should know. I think you'll need all the help you can get. By the way, do they still make picallili in England? I haven't tasted it for years."

Sitting at my desk littered with drawings of the kitchen plan, I remembered how Ercolino had driven his Vespa down to the station to join Angela in waving me off. As I climbed on board, Angela pressed a small package into my hand. In it was a sandwich made with slices of prosciutto and a little carton of red wine with a straw. I'd never seen anything quite like it.

Angela's picnics. She had always made one for me whenever I left to go anywhere during all the time we had now known each other. That was one of the items on the 'things I'll miss' list I had made when I had been trying to decide whether or not to leave Italy – and say goodbye to my house. The two handwritten pages were still on the table next to my handbag, ready to put in the car as soon as Angela and Ercolino arrived to take me on the first leg of my final journey back to England. I glanced at the first one.

Things I won't miss:

1. *Not being able to turn on the toaster and an iron without blowing the entire electrical circuit.*
2. *Not having an electric blanket in winter.*
3. *Having to spend two hours to get a cheque cashed in the bank.*
4. *Being stared at if I walk into a bar and order a drink.*
5. *Going to a dinner party where everyone sees who can talk the loudest.*
6. *Having to sit next to the women, while all the men sit together at the other end and talk about football.*
7. *Lecherous men.*
8. *Being told that the food is uneatable in England.*
9. *Being told that it never stops raining in England.*

I'd made my mind up now. I turned to the now crumpled second list.

Things I'll miss:

1. *The sound of the house martins chattering first thing in the morning.*
2. *The taste of strawberry wine.*
3. *Bombing around the winding roads in my little Fiat 500.*

4. *Diving from my small rowing boat for a swim in Lake Piediluco.*
5. *Ercolino's malapropisms.*
6. *Angela's picnics.*
7. *My lovely house.*

The writing trailed off at this point and the ink from the felt tip had smudged. My hand was still damp from wiping my eyes. I glanced at my watch. Ten minutes to get everything ready, finish my packing and wash the kitchen floor again. There was no real logic in it, but I had to leave the house spotless. It was the least I could do after deciding to abandon it.

★★★

Thanks to my correspondence with Cesare, I had learned a whole new Italian vocabulary, far removed from anything I ever came across at university. *Pozzo nero* was the latest new term I had had to grapple with. I had looked it up in the Italian-English dictionary that I now kept on my desk next to my typewriter. Cesspit. I'd just had one put in apparently. To be honest, I wasn't that familiar with the word in English. Things seemed to be moving in the right direction.

"Call for you on extension nine dearie. It's someone foreign, I think." Caroline cupped her hand over the receiver on the other side of the newsroom. "Nice voice, I must say! I do hope this is a work related call dearie. I'm still waiting for that story on the dive bombing seagull attacks in Peacehaven."

It had been Cesare on the phone, and it was not good news. The planning authorities in Montebello had paid a visit to my house and slapped a ban on all work until further notice. An overzealous official had noticed that some stone steps had been built on the approach to the property, and these weren't covered by the blanket planning alterations that Cesare had registered when the builders started work on the interior.

I involuntarily clapped a hand to my forehead, before removing it quickly as it became clear I was being watched.

"So what on earth do I do now?" I hissed down the phone.

"Don't worry. It's nothing that can't be fixed. Haven't you heard of a *condono*? Here in Italy, everything can be forgiven if you know how to go about it." I hurriedly thumbed through my dictionary under the entries for c. *Condono: pardon or amnesty, especially for work undertaken without planning permission.*

"*Tranquilla.* I'll take care of it." Cesare's voice was reassuring. "I only told you as I knew you were hoping to have the house habitable by Christmas. That's out of the question now I'm afraid. But we can sort it out. Of course, we'll have to pay."

So much for Christmas. So much for the house-warming party. I glanced up at the clock above my desk to see how long before I could decently make an exit.

"Everything all right is it?" said Caroline, sidling up to my desk. "You're not thinking of going home yet I hope. You know how we hate clock watchers in this newsroom."

Caroline had not been the only person to notice the change since I had come back from Italy. My two brothers telephoned me regularly, barely disguising their concern over the disaster they were convinced was looming. Although we all lived in different parts of the country, we were even closer now that we only had each other. Charles was very aware that he was the head of the family, with all the responsibilities this entailed.

"I know you won't like this, but I just wondered if it might be a good idea for you to see a doctor," he blurted out in one of his evening phone calls.

"What kind of doctor? I'm perfectly well."

You could almost hear him summoning up his courage on the other end of the line.

"Well, maybe one that you can talk to about things, about your feelings," he ventured uncomfortably.

"You mean a psychiatrist?"

"Well it can't do any harm. You've always been a bit reckless, but even you must admit that you've been acting very strangely lately. And it can't be easy living on your own after all this time."

In a way, he was right. It wasn't much fun living by myself after spending seven years with the man everyone had expected me to marry. And I had lost my appetite for the job I had once enjoyed so much, for the place where I lived and for the everyday routine that I now found suffocating. My new house in the Umbrian hills was the best thing that had happened to me for longer than I could remember.

To quell my brothers' fears, I had invited them both down for dinner a few nights later at the Italian restaurant three doors away from my house in Brighton. It was owned by a kind-looking man from Calabria called Vito, who would often invite me over for a glass of wine and a plate of pasta while he prepared the dinner menu, his wife eyeing us attentively from the kitchen where she was rolling out sheets of *lasagne*.

The evening had not been a great success. I saw my brothers' anxious glances as I handed round the photographs of my house in San Massano. I had taken the shots the day after I bought it, and although I was enraptured every time I looked at them, it was clear they didn't have the same effect on my brothers. I quickly took the pictures back and stuffed them into the frayed envelope that now went everywhere with me. It seemed the right moment to break some more news. I had decided to hand in my notice at work, put some tenants in my house in Brighton and move out to Italy so that I could follow the renovation more closely.

At my leaving party, held, as was traditional, in the Eagle, the editor bought the first round of drinks before making a short speech. Earlier, in his office, he had offered to take me back if, as he put it ominously, "things don't work out."

"In fact, if you agree to come back in, let's say a year, I'll see if I can get some sort of retainer for you while you're away."

It was very tempting. Having an income, however small, would make all the difference. And it would be far less risky if there was a job to come back to.

"Thank you. But I can't make any promises about coming back. So it's better to make a clean break." The words had come out before I could stop them.

"But what are you going to do? How will you earn a living? What about your career?" Everyone knew that this busy evening paper was a stepping stone to Fleet Street, the holy grail for reporters.

Other people's reactions were not much more encouraging.

"Are you crazy? Turning down the offer of money and your job back? That doesn't happen often in this business." Mark the crime reporter was incredulous. But then he had a wife and three children, so he had a different outlook on life. His desk was next to mine and he would often punctuate his calls to police contacts about robberies with equally fraught ones about the latest emergency in his domestic life.

"So long as you're leaving because you want to. Not because you're running away." That was Flynn, one of the subs, who didn't say much, but was famous for his quiet words of wisdom.

"Oh Italy. Yes, lovely place. It's just a pity they are all such thieves!" That was my uncle – my uncle by marriage, as I always pointed out. His disapproval made me want to go even more.

"I so hope you're doing the right thing. You worked so hard to become a journalist and now it looks as if you're throwing it all away," said my younger brother Jamie as he drove me to the airport a month and a half later. He squeezed my hand. "By the way, I couldn't resist, so I went out there a few weeks ago to see for myself what kind of crazy adventure you are getting into. You are quite mad, but I have to admit, the place is beautiful. I met your friends by the way."

25

"Look out for Space Bog," he called out mysteriously as I wheeled my trolley towards security.

"Are you sure you're doing the right thing?" Angela was standing beside me. The kitchen floor was dry now. "You don't have to go, you know. It's not too late to change your mind."

"Better we stay here and have a nice lunch rather than go outside in this rain. We'll get as wet as a chicken." That was Ercolino, practical as ever.

Angela glanced at the pieces of paper, thrust carelessly aside when I had gone to let them in.

"You've left out the most important one of all from the things you'll miss," she said.

"Yes, all the wonderful dinners we would have had together," chipped in her husband. "How are you going to survive with all that bloody awful English food? You've already lost enough weight as it is."

"No, it's something else, and I think she knows what it is," said Angela quietly.

"Yes, it's Mario." I felt my eyelashes become damp once again. "But it's no good. It just wouldn't work. I've made my decision. Come on. Let's get the luggage into the car before I miss the train."

Chapter Two

The family sitting opposite me in the compartment didn't take long to start unpacking their picnic. The train had barely pulled out of Rome station when the mother, a short wiry woman, began opening tupperware boxes from a large zipped holdall she kept near her feet. She passed around bundles of food wrapped in paper napkins to her husband and each of her three children. Then just as she was about to sit down again she hesitated as if she had forgotten something, and got back up to extend a paper bag in my direction. It was filled with large round shapes which appeared to be covered in breadcrumbs.

"Go on. They're *arancini*. Made with rice, meat sauce and mozzarella. I made them myself," said the woman. She pressed one into my hand while her husband passed me a paper cup filled with red wine.

"You're not from around here are you *Signorina*? I can tell by the way you look. Nor are we for that matter. We're from Sicily."

That explained the accent, which was totally different from anything I had heard before. "Have another. There's plenty for everyone."

There certainly seemed to be. As each container was emptied, another would appear from the seemingly bottomless bag, and passed round to each member of the family, before being offered to me. There was no point in arguing, and it seemed a long time since my last meal. The early morning Kenya Airways flight I had taken cost half as much as Alitalia, but the food had not looked tempting.

The Sicilian family was on a long journey back to Milan, where the father worked in a factory. They had been home to spend a few days holiday in Catania. Between mouthfuls, they talked nonstop about who they had seen during their stay, where they had gone, and especially what they had eaten. They had been travelling all night.

I had been away for nearly four months, and it felt good to be back. The train had picked up speed now, but it was warm and I stood up to open a window and enjoy the feeling of cooler air against my skin. Abruptly, the window was slammed shut, and I turned to see a heavily built middle-aged lady who had been sitting in the corner.

"We can't have windows open. The draught will give us a dreadful chill," she said firmly. I struggled to understand the logic, but looking around the rest of the carriage I saw that the decision had been made. Even the friendly Sicilian family was nodding in agreement with the woman.

"Draughts are very dangerous," said the mother, wiping her brow with a cotton handkerchief drawn from a large handbag. "Especially if you have been eating."

There was little choice but to give in. It was less than an hour now to Terni and it wouldn't be long until I was back in San Massano. The train pulled into the station at last and I peeled my legs off the leather seat. The Sicilian man handed down my three heavy bags and, to my relief, I saw Angela and Ercolino walking towards me along the platform. They both gave me a hug and Ercolino started fussing in his mixed metaphor English.

"Why have you brought so much luggage?" he said. "How am I going to fit all that in my car? It's only small you know. Like me. Like her. You drive me round the bloody wall."

"Leave her in peace Ercolino," said Angela, giving him a soft slap on one cheek and a kiss on the other.

"It's so good to see you again. Come on, we're going back to our place for some lunch. You must be starving."

Angela led the way out to the side street where they had left Ercolino's car. It was indeed very small, a gleaming bright red Fiat 500. And seeing Angela and Ercolino next to it, all three seemed made for each other. I hadn't really noticed before, but both husband and wife were a full head shorter than I was and fitted into the miniature car perfectly. I climbed into the back and squeezed my bags next to me and onto my lap.

"I can't see a bloody thing out of the back," said Ercolino.

"Oh shut up. It's only a few minutes' drive." Angela turned round to look at me.

"He loves his *Cinquecento* you know. People keep offering to buy it but he won't sell it."

On the way, we passed the steelworks, which was, I now knew, the major source of employment in Terni.

"They used to make weapons here," said Ercolino. "Did you know that the gun used to shoot President Kennedy was made here in Terni?"

A few minutes later, Ercolino pulled up outside a row of one-storey buildings, all of which looked the same.

"Here we are," he said. "Welcome to our home."

"Ah, the Cinquecento. Do you remember the time you ran up all those fines with your Cinquecento, and I had to get my policeman friend to get them torn up?" Ercolino had taken the list from Angela now, and was looking at the things that I'd miss.

"What a bloody pain in the harse you've been." He reached into the tiny leather handbag that he wore on one shoulder and pulled out a paper handkerchief. "You know something? I'm glad you're leaving. You drive me up the bend."

"And what's this? What's a malaprop... you bloody English."

★★★

Angela had told me the story of how she and Ercolino had come to live in Italy after eloping to Sweden, where they had spent several years. Angela's father had never forgiven her for marrying the son of a poor Catholic family and had cut her out of his life, and though Ercolino's family had proved more understanding, they had very little to offer. Then Ercolino's father had died, and the pair had decided that they should come back to look after Ercolino's mother. They had moved into the cramped council house where Ercolino had lived as a boy. There were two small bedrooms, a kitchen and a living room to share between Angela, Ercolino and Mamma. Angela gave English lessons at home and spent the rest of the time looking after her mother-in-law, giving her a head-to-toe wash once a week, perched on a plastic stool under the shower in the tiny bathroom.

"It's not exactly what I was used to, but it's not that bad, and she's a great character," said Angela as she showed me around.

"The thing I long for more than anything is to have a bath. We've only got this small shower."

That reminded me, and I opened my bag to find the jar of picallili I had brought for Angela. For Ercolino, there was a book. He only read books in English, he had told me, and had a weakness for novels, the fatter the better, set in faraway places such as India. His favourites were ones that revolved around long dynasties, with tales of family quarrels. There was nowhere you could find anything like that in Terni.

Lunch was a big plate of pasta with clams cooked by Angela and eaten in their kitchen with Mamma at the head of the table, knocking back two tumblers of red wine in quick succession. She had no teeth, which made it difficult to understand much of what she said, but she smiled most of the time and would occasionally pat Angela's hand and mutter something that sounded like "*brava!*"

As lunch progressed, with Mamma doing full justice to a large dish of ham and melon, Angela and Ercolino filled me in on some of the news from the village. I still hadn't met most of the people they talked about, but by the end of the meal, it felt as if I had known them for years.

Settima had been seen down on the main road between Terni and Spoleto, selling bundles of wild asparagus, most of which had been picked from Generosa's land when she wasn't looking. Dario and Valentina had set the date for their wedding.

"Valentina is Benedetto and Caterina's daughter, and Dario works in a car body repair workshop," explained Angela. "He seems a very nice boy and they'll be getting married in the village."

"Well they don't have much choice do they?" quipped her husband. "Seeing that she's already got a cake in the oven."

The old man who lived in a wing of the house that I had bought had died. Cesare's builders had found him one morning when they arrived to do the rewiring. It had taken some time to contact his sons, who lived down in Terni and who hardly ever came to see him. There had been a small funeral attended by most of the villagers. Angela and Ercolino had gone too, walking behind the hearse to the cemetery, which was set in a shaded vale down a gravel path flanked by cypress trees. The other main news was that Fabrizio, an 18-year-old boy from the village, was waiting to see if he would be called up for his military service. And local elections were planned the following week.

"That should be a bloody fiasco," muttered Ercolino acidly.

San Massano was one of the few strongholds in Umbria to remain under the control of the right-of-centre Christian Democrat party that was strongly supported by the Catholic Church. As a card-carrying member of the Communist Party, taken by his father to sign up as soon as he was eligible, the affront was too much for Ercolino.

"Oh yes, and Primo wants to tarmac the part of the driveway that your houses both share," said Angela.

"I told him it would cost a fortune and he said it wouldn't be a problem as you must have lots of money. Everyone thinks you must be rich if you're foreign. Anyway, he's coming over to see you once you're up there, so you haven't got much time to think of an excuse. You'll meet his sweet wife Nadia too."

My heart sank as the implications of Primo's plan began to register. The rent from my house in Brighton would cover the mortgage there, and I had a few contacts to launch what I hoped would be a new career writing for newspapers from Italy. But I had no salary at all for the time being. The situation had not been helped by the news from Cesare shortly before I left that he had managed to get the local council to lift the ban on my building work through the good offices of a friend who sat on the planning committee. That was a huge relief, but the change of heart had come with a price tag of several hundred thousand lire. The balance in my current account was worryingly low. In any case, the idea of covering the drive with tarmac horrified me. I liked the uneven surface and the colour of the stones, which exactly matched the warm yellow and pink shade of the stonework on the house.

After coffee, with Ercolino's cup laced with a generous shot of grappa, he took me outside to show me what he said was a surprise. During one of our frequent telephone calls conducted from the newsroom whenever Caroline wasn't looking, I had asked him to keep his eye out for a car that I could use while I was here. San Massano was far too remote to be served by public transport. There, parked outside the back of Ercolino's house was a pale yellow Fiat 500, a *Cinquecento*, almost identical to his red one, if not quite so shiny. It even had a small sunroof and would be perfect for driving around these narrow country lanes.

"Watch where you put your bloody feet," he said as I climbed into the spotless car that he had spent all morning cleaning. "You'd better like the house too," he said. "It's time we went to see it."

Cesare and his building team had done an extraordinary job, transforming the old ruin into a building that looked as if it really could become a home one day. But there was still a daunting amount of work to be done, perhaps rather more than I had remembered. The walls were much as when I had last seen them, pale blue in most of the rooms, the plaster bulging in what looked like giant blisters. In several places, whole chunks had fallen away. The holes in the roof were gone, and so too were the gaping chasms in the floors of the sitting room and the main bedroom. But there were no floor tiles to cover the grey concrete put down by the builders. The bath I had heard so much about was now installed. Best of all, there was hot running water, powered by an electric boiler. I pressed a switch on the wall. The light came on.

"You see what bloody luxury you've got?" said Ercolino.

Our gaze fell simultaneously on a strange sight out in the garden. It was an old metal and plastic chair with a hole made through the seat. Silver paper had been wrapped around what was left, and a loo roll was propped on a stick lashed to the backrest.

"Space Bog!" I muttered, recognising it instantly. "My brother came out here a few weeks ago when there was still no bathroom."

"Oh yes, I met him all right," said Ercolino. "He's completely up the bend, just like you. It must run in the family."

The next morning I was wakened early by a loud knocking on the door. It had taken me some time to get to sleep, partly because my mind was still whirring from the excitement of spending the night in my house for the first time, and partly because of the discomfort. Although it was spring, it was still cold at night up in the hills and the thick stone walls would take a very long time to warm up again after all these years of neglect. And to think I had always thought of Italy as a hot country.

There was no heating, apart from the massive fireplace in the sitting room, which had a large hook fixed on an old chain to support a cauldron for cooking soup and pasta. I looked at my watch. It was still six o'clock. Who could be calling on me so early? The hammering became more insistent, and pulling on a jumper and a pair of jeans, I stumbled sleepily to the door.

"Who is it?" I shouted, before drawing the ancient brass bolt that closed it from within. The faint sound of singing appeared to be coming from the other side. As I listened, it grew louder. It was a man's voice, and though it was hard to make out the words, they seemed to be in rhyme. I opened the door slowly and saw a face I recognised from the village. His hands clutched a basket containing about a dozen eggs and his eyes were half-closed as if in a trance. He was crooning a song in a strong dialect.

This was Pompeo, the gentle village troubadour or *cantastoria*. Aside from making up songs to tell the story of the people he knew, he spent most of his time having arguments with his wife Settima and seeking solace in the wine he produced from the strip of vines he kept on a small plot near his house. I strained to make out the words he was singing. The song seemed to be about a young woman from far away, who left her home to live with strangers. It wasn't easy to understand, not least because, as I now saw, Pompeo had tears slowly coursing down his cheeks. There was a faint reek of wine on his breath.

"I brought you a small gift, and I hoped you would do me the favour of taking me down to Montebello," he said. He wiped his face with the back of his sleeve. "I have to run a few errands, and there are so few people here who have a car."

I had only had my *Cinquecento* since the previous afternoon. News clearly got around fast in these parts. Pompeo's features dissolved into more tears, and I guessed that there must have been another altercation with Settima. She was far from beautiful, with thin wiry hair that had been inexpertly dyed at home, and several teeth missing. But rumour had it that she was a woman of easy virtue, popular with some of the older men in the nearby villages and that she accepted presents in return for her favours. Since the family home lacked most things, she encouraged her admirers to give her practical gifts.

The previous evening, Pompeo had come home from the fields to find Settima cooking dinner with a brand new set of gleaming pots and pans. It didn't take him long to work out where they had come from, and the villagers sitting around in the piazza had suddenly witnessed a volley of frying pans and saucepans come shooting from Settima's kitchen window, amid much shouting from within. The offending cooking utensils had subsequently disappeared from where they had fallen. No one could say exactly what had happened to them, but Generosa, a buxom woman in her sixties with a reputation as one of the sharpest characters in the village, had been seen carrying a large bundle as she slipped into her front door shortly before midnight.

This morning, Pompeo was adamant that he needed to go to Montebello and, now that I was up, I saw no reason not to take him. I hadn't had a chance to get in any supplies, so it would be a good opportunity to pick up some bread, cheese and wine. For the time being, I had no way of making anything warm, unless I made up the fire in the sitting room to cook on. Pompeo asked to be dropped off at the *carabinieri*, the local police station for the surrounding area.

I arranged to meet him an hour later after I had been to the small grocery store just around the corner. The sign outside claimed it was a *supermercato*, but aside from the usual salames, cheeses and sides of prosciutto displayed behind a glass counter, the only products it seemed to sell were flowered overalls for women to put over their dresses as they went about their household chores and hobnail boots for both men and women to wear as they worked in the fields.

Pompeo was quiet on the way home, though he muttered something I didn't catch as he climbed into the front seat. I was keen to get back to see Benedetto, the villager recommended by Cesare. There was still so much to be done inside the house that it was difficult to know where to begin. The walls needed stripping of the old paint and plaster before being given a fresh coat of whitewash. For some unfathomable reason, the wooden beams that crisscrossed each ceiling had been covered with layers of the ubiquitous pale blue paint at some stage, so they would also need to be stripped and restained. I had no fridge, no cupboards and almost no furniture, aside from a rusty old bed that had been left in the cellar. There was also a formica covered table in the kitchen, complete with a drawer filled with tin knives and forks. The outside area was a seething mass of brambles which were gradually strangling the olive trees that dotted the terraced slopes.

Pompeo said he would send Benedetto down. He climbed out of the car and thanked me again for the lift, his mood definitely more upbeat now. Back inside my house, I reached into the drawer of the kitchen table to retrieve a menacing looking knife that I had spotted earlier. This was just what I needed to hack a piece of bread from the loaf I had just bought. Although the bread was freshly made that morning, it was no easy task cutting off a slice. The crust was thick and hard and the inside was firm and strangely tasteless. As I had already discovered, the local bread was one of the more unappetising features of Umbrian cuisine, though it did make delicious *bruschetta*, once grilled over the fire and topped with garlic, olive oil and a sprinkle of salt. Salt was the missing ingredient. The bread around here was made without it, a hangover from the Salt Wars some four centuries earlier between the city states allied to Perugia and Spoleto, and the others who sided with the Vatican. I had read all about the conflict in a book that Mirella had given me as a present when I decided to buy the house.

"In many ways, not much has changed," she had said as I unwrapped the book. Mercifully, she had given up trying to speak in English. "Most of the small fortress hill towns have a long and bloody history of fighting amongst each other. They all still hate each other's guts, and San Massano is no exception."

There was no point in putting it off any longer. There was work to be done. I still hadn't unpacked as there was nowhere to put anything, so reaching for one of my bags, I pulled out a pair of shorts and one of my brother's old rugby shirts. There were some rubber gloves to protect my hands and a ski hat and goggles to keep the worst of the old paint out of my eyes and hair. Just as well there no mirrors yet, I thought. I dragged the kitchen table into what I had decided would be my bedroom, and climbed up to see if I could reach the ceiling from there. Not quite. A chair like the one that had been dismembered to make Space Bog should do the trick, though it was pretty precarious. Armed with a scraper and a steel brush I had bought down in Montebello, I began to hack away at the layers of old blue paint. It came away quite easily, and I soon worked out the best way of using first the scraper then the brush to reveal the wood of the beams. But it was painfully slow. And it was very uncomfortable working at that angle. Now I knew how Michelangelo felt when he painted the Sistine Chapel.

The put-put sound of an engine interrupted my musings, and I looked out of the window to see an *Ape* – a Bee — chugging up the drive. That was the name aptly given to the noisy but zippy contraptions that seemed to serve as transport for many of the villagers in this part of Umbria. Just the thing really, for these narrow roads. Mirella had told me there had been no road at all to San Massano until twenty five years ago. The only thing that connected the village to the outside world has been a dirt track which most people had travelled by mule. Progress had brought with it a wider path, which was actually paved in some parts, but it was still not suited to cars of any great size.

The *Ape* drew to a halt, and a short swarthy man climbed out from a bench seat, turning off the engine beneath what looked like the handlebars of a motor scooter. Hanging from the leather belt pulled tight beneath a large stomach was a chilling assortment of cutting tools, among them a knife, a scythe and what appeared to be a small saw. From the other side, a woman with greying hair and pebble glasses stepped out and stood beside him, coughing every now and then. She was wearing one of the pinafores and a pair of the boots I had seen in the shop that morning.

The couple needed little introduction, and I knew from their appearance that this must be Benedetto and his wife Caterina. Angela had told me over lunch the previous day that the couple had been married for twelve years and had twin boys of about the same age. But Caterina had six other older children, all of them by different fathers.

"Everyone thinks of Italians as being very religious and obeying the Church," Angela had said. "Of course it's all nonsense. They're a licentious bunch, especially up here. I suppose it's because there's not much else to do. They're always either at it, or talking about it, as far as I can see."

Benedetto, Caterina and I went through the ritual of formally introducing ourselves and shaking hands, and I noticed that Benedetto was missing the ends of a couple of fingers. I started to explain what kind of work I needed doing, and he interrupted me, saying something that I struggled to understand. His wife uttered a few words of explanation, though it was impossible to grasp much of what she was saying either. Benedetto now started to speak even faster, in an animated way, smiling broadly, his eyes shining meaningfully. Caterina broke into a laugh and they both looked at me expectantly. It appeared that Benedetto had just made a joke, but I hadn't a clue what it was. It wasn't just the accent that threw me, or the machine gun speed of the delivery of their speech. The dialect these people used was quite another language, with completely different words. Benedetto was especially hard to understand, though he clearly found the whole thing highly amusing. So much for my university degree. I could read Petrarch's poetry and discuss the allegory in Dante's Inferno, but I couldn't hold a sensible conversation with the people who were now my neighbours.

We moved inside so that I could show Benedetto around and we could discuss where shelves would go once the walls had been scraped and repainted. We entered the kitchen and Caterina smiled wistfully.

"This was where I went to school. My desk was just here and the teacher used to stand over there by the blackboard," she said, helping me to understand with plenty of gestures, and pointing to what was now the sink. I remembered what Mirella had told me that first time I saw it, that the house had once served as the village school, all the classes mixed in together in the one room. Nowadays, the children went down in a rickety old school bus to Montebello, driven at breakneck speed by Ettore, who lived with his old mother.

We went outside to a courtyard where I wanted to make a *pergola* with some vines. I asked Benedetto if he could do it, and with the help of Caterina, we worked out that he would cut some young oak trees from the wood behind the property and strip them of their bark to make a canopy. Then he would take his *Ape* down to Montebello and buy some vines to plant.

"But for the planting, I'll have to wait till the moon is on the rise, so they'll have a better chance of taking," he said.

"Why is that?" I had kept a small garden back in Brighton, but I'd never taken any notice of the moon.

"Because young plants do much better if you put them in when the moon is getting bigger, than if you do when it's getting smaller. It's Nature," he replied. To him, it seemed painfully obvious.

The amount of work Benedetto was going to do was building up, so I pulled out a piece of paper from my pocket and started to jot down some of the things he would need to buy.

"I'll just remember them. I'll need about 50 strong nails, 40 metres of wire, six young vines, and a 50 kilo bag of soil. Then I'll need some timber for the shelves and some brackets to hold them up." Benedetto reeled off other things he would need, and I wrote them down on the piece of paper before handing him the list.

"No no, I don't need that," he said emphatically, and pushed the paper away. It wasn't until he had obstinately refused my third attempt to give him the list that the truth at last dawned on me. How stupid I had been. Benedetto could not read or write.

Before the couple climbed into their *Ape* to go home, Caterina invited me to their house for dinner that evening.

"You can meet the rest of our family," she said. "Cooking for one more person won't make any difference."

"*Signorina CLAY!*" A woman's high-pitched voice shrieked over the chug of Benedetto's engine, making us all turn round to see where it was coming from.

"Come over HERE!"

"*Oh dio*. It's Nadia, Primo's wife." Benedetto had a mischievous smile on his face.

"They're your neighbours. You'd better go and see what she wants. I'm off, or I'll never get anything done. Good luck."

Caterina was smiling too and waved briefly as the *Ape* careered full pelt down the bumpy driveway.

"*Signorina Clay!* Over here."

A tall slim woman with bobbed hair liberally streaked with bright blonde highlights was beckoning energetically from the other side of the fence that divided my house from the next door property.

"*Piacere.* How do you do. I'm Nadia. I've been wanting to meet you." She stretched out a well manicured hand with dark pink nails and coloured bangles that rattled as she moved. Her handshake was limp and soft, which was just as well given the assortment of chunky gold rings that adorned her fingers.

"I wanted to invite you over to show you my house. Come on, I'll make you a coffee. I buy the beans in the Bar Sant'Eustachio in Rome. Whatever made you buy a place in this god forsaken hole?"

Barely pausing to draw breath, she led the way up the drive to a modern house with pink walls. The property, which was hidden from view behind thick laurel bushes, was imposing in its way, with what appeared to be a great many rooms, a wide terrace edged with severe iron railings and a garden filled with formal shrubs and elaborate lampposts made of wrought iron, with a glass bobble on the top like a spaceman's helmet.

"I found those lamps at a garden centre in Rome," she said, pushing open the front door to reveal a gleaming parquet floor.

"You won't find anything like that around here – in this area you only get shops that cater for peasants."

"So how are you finding it here?" She was now leading me into a kitchen with red cupboards so shiny that you could see your reflection. She reached up to a cabinet with a golden sheen to its glass front and pulled out a large coffee pot.

"I can't think why you like it here. I'd be scared stiff all on my own. I can't wait to get down to the coast at Nettuno as soon as we've finished here with our duty visit, seeing Primo's mother and checking on the dogs. Though between you and me, it's the dogs he's more interested in." She leaned a little closer and lowered her voice slightly, apparently oblivious that she was still speaking loudly enough for just about anyone to hear within a hundred yard range.

"They're hunting dogs you know, and they're worth quite a bit. And you can't really blame Primo for not paying that much attention to the old lady. Not after what she did to him when he was such a young boy. *Povero tesoro.*"

Nadia handed me a small cup of coffee and pushed over a glass canister of sugar with a gilt spout.

"How many teaspoons, two or three? I'll just have one as I've got to watch my weight." She smoothed her hands over a flat stomach under a tight purple skirt which she wore with matching high-heeled suede ankle boots. "It'll soon be time to put my bikini on down in Nettuno. Our house is right near the beach you know. You should come and see us. It would give you a bit of a break from this dump."

The sound of a back door opening halted Nadia's description of the house in Nettuno, the restaurants that served such good fish, the sun loungers and umbrellas that she rented for the season, the hairdresser who knew just how she liked her fringe cut, and did a special conditioner to counter the effect of all that sun and saltwater on her hair.

"Oh *ciao tesoro*. You're back. Look, it's Clay, our next door neighbour. We were just having a chat about girls' things, but I know you wanted to talk to her about the drive and the damage that those potholes are doing to the Mercedes. Here, there's a coffee for you *tesoro*, but do wash your hands if you've been touching those dogs."

Primo's obviously expensive shirt was unbuttoned half-way down his chest to reveal several thick gold chains. He went to the sink and washed his hands obediently, while Nadia stood by with a pink fluffy towel. He turned to greet me.

"Nadia's probably told you that we want to resurface the drive," he said, getting straight to the point that I was equally anxious to avoid. "The lower part of the drive serves both houses, so we'd share the cost. I've already got an estimate and it would come to about a million lire. So your share would be five hundred thousand."

"We could get some more of those lampposts from Rome

and run a line of them up the drive. It would look rather striking," his wife chipped in.

Keen to change the subject I asked if Primo's mother lived with them. It was Nadia who answered.

"Oh no, she still lives in her little house up in the village. She wouldn't like it down here." She took a step closer to her husband and placed her hand on his forearm possessively. "She doesn't mind the stink of pigs and sheep. Can you believe it? They still keep their animals in their houses with them," Nadia said. She was carefully stacking the tiny coffee cups into a dishwasher behind one of the gleaming red doors.

"You know that's not really fair Nadia. It's just what people are used to round here," said Primo. "In San Massano, most people live in the upper part of the houses and the lower part is used to keep the cows, sheep, goats and chickens. It keeps the houses warm in winter."

"Yes, and it means that everywhere is crawling with flies in the summer," said Nadia. "You can't imagine the smell." She gave a shudder. I seized on the slight rift to made my exit from Primo and Nadia's house, promising to give some more thought to the idea of the tarmac, though inwardly determined to do no such thing.

"So what did the *Principessa* have to say for herself?" Benedetto was seated at a long wooden table in a dark room with a fireplace at one end when I knocked on the half-opened door several hours later.

"I bet she told you that we are all peasants."

"She's not so bad Benedetto. Just a bit stuck up." Caterina was crouched in the corner near the fireplace, bent over a pile of thick slices of bread that she was arranging on a double-sided wire rack. She snapped it shut and placed it over the embers.

"I can't think what he saw in her. Just because he made some

43

money he had to go and marry a blonde floozy like that. And from Rome!"

"Sit yourself down," Caterina removed the now toasted bread from the rack and doused each piece with thick green olive oil from a glass bottle with no label.

"Here, have some *bruschetta*." She placed a thick chunk of toasted bread soused with oil on a paper napkin in front of me.

The rest of the large family was already seated, and one by one they stood up shyly to shake my hand. The eldest boy, Pietro, was not there this evening. His place at table was taken by a fresh-faced young man from a neighbouring village. This was Dario, who had a good job in a car body repair shop down in Terni, said Caterina, moving around the table with the plate of *bruschetta*. Next to him was one of the daughters, a pretty girl called Valentina, with a slight bump showing on her stomach.

The twins sat next to Benedetto, one on each side, and he carefully carved them fine slices of *salame* from the knife he had unhooked from his belt. The boys were not hard to tell apart. The smaller of the two, Giovanni, was very slight, his skinny legs squeezed into a pair of dirty trousers, with tousled brown hair falling over a wide-eyed face that bore an expression of permanent surprise. His brother Luca was of a sturdier build, more like his father. His face was dominated by a long nose that appeared to start from his forehead, with one eye slightly higher than the other.

"It was hard work today. I had to get old Bruno's lambs sorted for Easter and the biggest one just wouldn't play the game." Benedetto smiled and drew his thumb across his neck. As well as doing various odd jobs, he slaughtered pigs and lambs for local families. "Still, I got him in the end. Fair did my back in today, with all that bending over. Pass me another *bruschetta* Caterina."

Caterina was bent over the fire to prod some sausages that were cooking on the red hot ash. Every so often, she drew some more ash from beneath the flaming logs that were propped up against the rear of the hearth. Her hacking cough seemed to be worse this evening. She got up to serve Benedetto some more *bruschetta*. Benedetto helped himself to a large glass of wine from a plain glass flask and passed the bottle over to me.

"I made this myself," he said. "It comes from the *fragolino* grape. Tastes like strawberries, but they say it makes you mad if you drink too much of it."

As ever, it took me a while to decipher what he was saying, but I sipped the pale red liquid with its faint taste of strawberries and accepted a slice of *salame* extended from the point of Benedetto's knife.

"If you like, I'll plant one of these vines in your *pergola*. Then you can be mad too," he said, laughing loudly. The rest of the family took the cue and joined in with the laughter. Loudest of all was Caterina, though her mirth was punctuated by more and more frequent bursts of coughing as the wood smoke choked her lungs.

"It's Friday. Ercolino and Angela will have got here by now." Caterina was passing round a plate piled high with sausages. You wouldn't want to be a vegetarian in this household, I reflected, slicing one open to reveal dark red meat flecked with small lumps of white fat. "Luca, go and call them over. They can have some sausages if they haven't already eaten.

"Good aren't they?" she turned to me offering another sausage from the plate. "We make them from our pigs. It's the liver that gives them that nice strong flavour."

It took less than five minutes to retrieve Ercolino and Angela from their house next door, where they had been lighting the fire to warm the place up.

"I suppose you've been giving it a good poke," said Benedetto, reaching out to pour a glass of *fragolino* wine for Angela and Ercolino.

Everyone roared with laughter.

"Oh yes, and we've been sweeping ever since we got here. It's the only way to keep warm," said Ercolino, giggling. He drew up a chair close to the fire.

More laughter. Dario was almost crying by now, and Caterina was spluttering and coughing as she handed the two newest arrivals a couple of plates and some freshly cooked sausages.

"Don't take any notice of them," said Angela. She sat down next to me. But you could tell she thought it was funny too.

"They've got one track minds. That's all they ever think about."

"You see, the word for poke in dialect means something else too. And so does sweep," said Ercolino helpfully. "In fact, pretty much everything's got a double meaning. You'll soon get the hang of it."

"So tell us about your meeting with Primo and the lovely Nadia." Benedetto raised his eyes to heaven theatrically at the mention of her, and held out his knife threateningly.

"I'd soon sort her out, just like I do with the lambs."

"Primo would be very sad. And after all, he is your cousin," Ercolino pointed out. "So he's Caterina's cousin too."

"Benedetto and Caterina are first cousins," Angela whispered by way of explanation. "In those days, it wasn't against the law to marry your cousin. Everyone is related around here."

I asked the question that had been intriguing me ever since Nadia had first mentioned it. What had Primo's mother done that was so dreadful?

Benedetto began to explain, but mercifully Ercolino stepped in and took up the story.

"Primo's family was one of the poorest in the village, and, with nine children, there just wasn't enough food to go round. Primo was the eldest – that's why he was called Primo – and when he reached thirteen, his mother gave him his bus fare to Rome, and told him she was sorry, but they couldn't afford to keep him anymore."

He reached for a second glass of wine and stabbed another sausage on his fork.

"After a while, he managed to find a job as a baker's boy, running errands and making deliveries on a bike. He'd never so much as seen a bicycle in San Massano. He was given a small weekly wage and a bed to sleep on next to the bread oven. It must have been very tough."

"But these days he owns a chain of bakeries, and can afford just about anything he likes, so..." said Caterina, standing up from the fireplace and planting the fist of her right arm firmly into the crook of her left arm in a gesture that left no shadow of a doubt as to its meaning. "He loves hunting, especially wild boar, and he comes back to say hello to all of us, but he doesn't spend much time at his mother's place, though she's nearly eighty now. I suppose you can't really blame him."

The glow from Benedetto's strawberry wine did much to ward off the worst of the chill as I climbed into bed much later that night. Pulling the blankets closer around me, I wondered idly what Carla would have made of this evening. At school, she had always made it clear that she was from a good middle class family that came from well-heeled Ferrara. The only girl who failed to thrive under Carla's wing had been called Maria, and surprisingly, she was Italian. To be precise, she was half-Sicilian, and wore earrings, though jewellery was banned at school. If Maria put her hand up in class, you could be sure her answer would be wrong, even though it sounded impressively authentic to the rest of us. To be honest, Carla had been a dreadful snob.

It was my headache that woke me next morning, that and the pain in my chest, which felt as if I was wearing a metal straitjacket that was being pulled tighter and tighter. I wondered what was wrong with me. There was no aspirin in the house, so I gingerly crawled out of bed and walked painfully up to the village. I would ask Caterina if she had anything. I had seen a well-stocked medicine cabinet and had watched her doling out some sort of syrup to the twins.

"You look dreadful, what's the matter?" said Caterina. She made a place for me at the kitchen table. She told me I should see a doctor. Maybe I had been sleeping in a draught or had drunk something too cold? I tried to protest on all fronts, but Caterina had already taken things into her own hands. Dr. Conti from Montebello was upstairs examining Benedetto's mother, who had problems with her heart. He could take a look at me on his way out.

The doctor's verdict, when it came, was hard to understand, but the gist of it appeared to be a chest infection. He got out his prescription pad and scribbled something illegible on one of the sheets. Some things are the same the world over, I thought. The cure, however, was not something I was ready for.

"You will need two injections for seven days, and you will need to use one of these suppositories, once a day until you are feeling better." He pulled various boxes out of his bag and presented me with a bill for 50,000 lire.

"Generosa can do the injections. She does them for everyone in the village," said Caterina. "I'll call her now. I just saw her out in the yard killing some of her chickens."

Generosa arrived a few minutes later. Her hair had several feathers in it and there were a few spots of blood on her pinafore.

"Here *Stellina*, give me the phial and hold out your arm. This won't take a second." She reached out a grimy hand that clutched a plastic syringe. Suddenly I felt much much better, and mumbling something about having to write an important article, I rushed out of the door. In the piazza, as I headed quickly for the sanctuary of my house, I almost bumped into Tito.

"Ah, *Signorina*, I'm so glad that I've met you," he said, smiling broadly. "I'd like you to be one of the first people to know. I have some important news."

Chapter Three

Tito's impending marriage was the talk of the village. Being a practical person and always careful with his money, he had taken the precaution of wooing the woman he had decided to marry from a distance. The whole relationship had been conducted through the offices of his cousin, Rinaldo. The cousin lived in the same village as the lady who had been identified by both men as the perfect match for Tito. Clara had been a nun since the age of 18, a natural choice given the straitened family circumstances and the presence of eight brothers and sisters. But now, well into her forties, with her parents long dead, she had changed her mind and resolved to see what life had to offer outside the walls of the convent that had been home for almost as long as she could remember. Her brothers and sisters were all married, with families of their own, so Clara faced an uncertain future, with no one to support her. The remote village to which she had returned was 50 km from San Massano, across a mountain range connected only by an unpaved road. It was a long trip for Tito to make, though he was desperately anxious to see what she looked like after Rinaldo spoke of her during a visit back to the village where he had grown up.

The two men had talked long into the night and made a plan that seemed certain to answer everyone's needs. After making overtures to Clara on Tito's behalf, the cousin embarked on a proxy courtship, paying her visits and taking her flowers or little cakes, meticulously noting the cost in a notebook he kept in his pocket, for Tito had promised to reimburse him later. Once a week, at a pre-arranged time, Tito and Clara spoke by telephone, Tito dialling from the cabin at the back of his shop, the only phone in San Massano, and Clara waiting for the call in the village café, which had the only phone for miles around. In the background, Rinaldo waited, nursing a coffee and with a cup of sugared *orzo*, the cost duly noted, ready for Clara as soon as she emerged from her booth.

After two months, certain that he had found the right person at last, Tito woke at dawn one Sunday morning, polished his car, an old but immaculately kept small version of a station wagon that looked as if it would be worth a fortune in a veteran car collection. When he was satisfied with the shine, he got in, lightly touched the magnetic crucifix that he kept on the dashboard and drove carefully over the mountains to meet Clara. She had a round, pleasant face, framed by black hair greying at the temples, worn short after years of being covered by a veil. She was well built, not thin and bony, but not overweight either. She would fit perfectly into Tito's bed back in San Massano and the couple would keep each other warm in the long winter nights. Shortly after lunch, he proposed to her. She immediately accepted, as he knew she would.

"You must have been very sure that you were going to like her," I said when he told me the news in the piazza outside his shop. He had got back the previous evening, and had an uncharacteristic glow to his usually pale cheeks.

"You don't think I was going to waste all that petrol driving there and back for nothing," he retorted.

"Does the *Signorina* have a family?" The question was not directed at me, even though I was the subject of the inquiry and was sitting at a table laden with food amongst the family who had invited me to lunch. It was becoming increasingly obvious that I was something of a novelty, and invitations like today's were not uncommon. Grazia, the hostess, looked past me towards Angela and Ercolino. They had clearly taken on the status of my parents, at least for this particular occasion, given that it appeared I did not have any of my own.

I saw Natalino, the son, shift uncomfortably in his chair as his mother leaned over his shoulder and ladled out a large helping of *strangozzi* with wild asparagus. She passed to my place, which had been set strategically next to Natalino's, still refusing to catch my eye.

"Does the *Signorina* like home-made pasta?" she asked Ercolino. "I made it myself with our own olive oil. The asparagus come from the hills around the village."

I assured her that I did, but she seemed not to hear me. My stand-in parents confirmed what I had said and Grazia spooned some pasta into my plate before moving on to serve the rest of the large gathering seated around the old wooden table. I waited for her to sit down, but everyone else plunged their forks into their pasta and started eating noisily. Grazia, a thin, severe looking woman with the regulation overall fitted tightly over a high-necked dark brown dress, made no move to take her place, but turned towards the waist-high fireplace, which was lit in spite of the warm temperature outside. She piled some hot ash over a dish of pizza stuffed with spinach and covered with silver foil. While she waited for it to finish cooking, she used her fingers to turn some lamb chops on the griddle placed over the embers.

"These are from our own lambs," she said, still speaking to Angela and Ercolino, though the information seemed to be aimed at me. "We've got sheep, five cows, chickens, olives, vines. And of course, a truffle hunting dog."

"You won't go hungry here," interjected Natale, the grandfather, smiling toothlessly as he attempted to chew some meat from the lamb chop that his daughter-in-law had just put on his plate. Natalino put down his food and darted a meaningful glance in the direction of the old man.

51

"And does the *Signorina* have a boyfriend?" inquired Grazia, as though the idea had only just come to her.

"Why not take Natalino?" asked the grandfather loudly, nudging me vigorously. The table went quiet as Natalino visibly shrank in his chair.

"I'm so sorry about all this," he muttered under his breath.

Poor Natalino had not had the best of days and I couldn't help feeling sorry for him. Earlier he had borrowed his father's car to take me to a tiny lake suspended in the mountains, which was reached by a seemingly endless series of unpaved roads that wound up through the soft green hills. The sun was warm and when we reached the narrow stretch of grass next to the lake, I stripped down to my swimming costume under my shorts and tee-shirt.

"Aren't you coming in?" I asked, heading for the water. He looked down uncertainly at his short pale legs, having reluctantly removed his trousers.

"I am as white as a mozzarella," he said. "I'll stay here and get some sun and watch you swim instead."

There was no persuading Natalino to come into the water, for, as he confessed shyly when I emerged ten minutes later, he had never learned how to swim. He had another confession to make, which was even more difficult, though not entirely unexpected. He was definitely not my type, so I tried to explain that I was not looking for any kind of relationship, other than friendship of course. It was becoming increasingly clear that life in San Massano was going to be more complicated than I had thought.

However embarrassing Natalino may have found the lunch with his family, the banquet that his mother had served offered me a welcome respite from my usual diet of tasteless bread and cheese. I certainly didn't have the patience to light the fire like Caterina every time I needed to eat or have a cup of tea, and I didn't want to end up with a hacking cough like hers from the smoke. There was no such thing as an electric kettle in the shops round here, though I made a mental note to put one in my suitcase on my next trip back from England. Come to think of it, I had yet to see a washing machine. The village women all washed their clothes at the fountain in the piazza. Picturesque though the scene might be, it was not for me and I resolved to pay a visit to Terni to buy a stove and some other essential things such as a sofa and some chairs.

Ercolino said he knew a store that sometimes had good deals, and suggested we go and take a look. He would leave Mamma at home in front of her favourite soap opera – Hart to Hart, which became 'Art a 'Art without the aitches when dubbed into Italian – then both he and Angela would be free to come with me. Knowing that the temperature would be much warmer in Terni, which was right down in the valley, I put on a pair of shorts and drove to meet them.

"Why are you wearing bloody shorts?" said Ercolino, when I got out at the petrol station he had chosen as the meeting place. "You look as if you're going to the beach."

Ercolino was stirring a coffee laced with *sambuca*, though it was only half-past ten. Every filling station around here seemed to have a bar attached to it, and he and Angela were waiting at a table outside.

"Don't be so old-fashioned," said Angela, patting his shoulder affectionately. "All the young people in England wear shorts once it gets a bit warmer." I had a cappuccino, though it came as no real surprise that it was the wrong choice.

"*Porco Dio*! In Italy you only drink cappuccino first thing in the morning," said Ercolino, throwing up his hands in exasperation. "After that, you have to drink espresso, with no milk. You bloody English don't understand a thing."

The furniture showroom was in the centre of town, up a narrow side street. In the windows were some dining chairs made to an unmistakable Italian design. With straight backs made of intricately worked wrought iron, the seats were cushioned with a pale cream fabric, tied loosely at the rear with an elegant sash. Behind them was a thick glass-topped dining table supported by pillars carved out of yellow marble.

"Don't worry, I know this place," said Ercolino seeing my look of concern as I examined the price tag.

The owner was a tall man in his late fifties, who recognised Ercolino and shook hands with all of us. He had just what the *signorina* needed, he said, leading the way to another room. In it was a dark caramel coloured sofa made out of the softest Italian leather, flanked by two matching armchairs. They would look perfect around my fireplace. The shop owner invited me to try them out, and I settled into one of the armchairs, while Angela and Ercolino sat on the sofa. The conversation turned to the house I had bought. Like everyone, it seemed, the owner wanted to know if I was with my parents and, if not, was I married? On hearing that I was on my own he raised his eyebrows. The price was agreed, a much lower one than I had feared, since the furniture had been repossessed from someone who had been unable to keep up with his payments. I wrote out the cheque and the shopkeeper emerged from another room with a bottle of white wine and four glasses.

"Let us drink to your new home," he said, raising his glass towards me. "And to a very happy life among your friends here in Italy."

Outside the store, Angela and I chatted about how best to arrange the furniture once it was delivered. Ercolino had stayed behind to talk to the store owner, though he seemed to be taking a long time. At last he emerged, looking vaguely troubled.

"What is it Ercolino? I can see something's the matter," said his wife.

Ercolino raised his arms above his head in a dramatic gesture that I had come to interpret as meaning something serious.

"*Madonna santa*, it's those bloody shorts. I knew she should never have worn them." He was so agitated that it took several minutes to calm him down and make him explain. When he was able to speak, Ercolino recounted that the shopkeeper had called him back and asked him if he could have a word. He wanted to know if the blonde *signorina* would like to spend a few days with him. After all, she was all alone and it was nearly Easter. He could get away from his wife and maybe take the young lady to the coast to show her some of the beautiful beaches Italy had to offer.

"So what did you say to him?" asked Angela.

"I told him that he was a bloody disgrace to Italy," said Ercolino, who was by now almost in tears at the affront. "And I told him that if he ever tried to do anything like that again, I'd kick him somewhere it really hurts – right in the nutknackers."

On the way home, a now slightly calmer Ercolino stopped at a shop which sold household appliances. There was no electric kettle, of course, but I found a basic cooker that had four rings and an oven, and arranged for it to be sent up the same day. Now I would have to get a gas canister brought up by Tito. The cooker was powered by gas, but like most of the villages in the area, San Massano was still not connected to the mains supply.

Tito was in his shop when I got back to the village, humming quietly to himself. He was going through his daily ritual of rearranging his few wares on the shelves. A quick glance around the store revealed a few loaves of the usual bread, some tired looking ham and an assortment of red candles decorated with the face of Padre Pio, a monk who had had stigmata on the palms of his hands before he died and who was much revered around here. The shopkeeper promised to bring the canister down first thing the next morning.

True to his word, Tito drove up my drive soon after nine o'clock the following day. He heaved the canister out of the rear of his car, still dusty from its long drive over the mountains, and propped it on his shoulder, following me up the steep stone stairs to the front door of the house.

"You've done a good job here." He set the large gas bottle down and hooked up a rubber tube to the cooker that had been delivered earlier. "But you do really need a man about the house to do the heavy work like this. Everyone needs company in life." Tito had no change for the 25,000 lire note I proffered him, so he waved it aside and said I could pay later.

"I'm open until lunchtime, so you can drop by any time," he said. "After that, I have my weekly phone call to Clara, and we've decided to talk for ten minutes this time, instead of the usual five. There's so much to plan before we get married in October." He went out, humming the same tune I had heard earlier.

With Tito gone, I decided to make a start on the painting. I had finished the worst of scraping off the old paint from the walls and the beams, though my knuckles were now raw and my neck ached. The next phase would be to whitewash the walls and stain the beams with a curious solution of crumbled walnut shells that Cesare had told me I would find in a hardware store in Terni. He had offered to send in decorators to do the job, and when I told him that I was quite happy to do it myself he looked at me curiously. I had bought three big drums of whitewash and several paintbrushes of various sizes at the same store. After covering the floor with old copies of *Il Corriere della Sera*, I was soon slapping paint on the walls of the main bedroom. The radio I had brought with me from England was turned up loud to a local station, *Radio Subasio*, which blared out sugary Italian pop music punctuated by adverts for local businesses.

"Buy two, get three at *Zuperconti*. An Easter egg for all the family. Each one with a surprise in the centre!" boomed out a woman's seductive voice between jingles.

"Spring is here, and so are the chicks. Come and get yours now at Di Paolo's and you'll be cluck, cluck, clucking all the way to the dinner table."

I was rather enjoying myself, and resolved to paint a wall a day. That should take care of the worst of the decorating by the time the real heat of the summer arrived. It was Good Friday tomorrow, I realised suddenly. Dragging the big tin of whitewash further along the wall, I heard what sounded like a knock on the door. Who could that be? I wasn't expecting anyone and there was still half a wall to be finished before I could knock off for the day. "Come in," I yelled.

"*Permesso?*" asked a voice I didn't recognise. I did recognise the face, however. It belonged to a man who owned a restaurant in the village of Fiore, a few miles from San Massano, where I had been for dinner one evening with Cesare and Mirella. The visitor, who looked as if he was in his mid-fifties, held a small bouquet of flowers out towards me, where I stood on the chair, my hands covered in paint. He had decided to pay a visit to see how the house was coming on, he said awkwardly. Then, just as awkwardly, he made a clumsy lunge.

"Just a little kiss," he said. "You must be lonely here all by yourself. We could keep each other company."

Torn between outrage and laughter, I ordered the man out of the house and watched him scurry down the drive to his car, which was parked at the bottom.

The lechers. Well I certainly wouldn't miss them. For some reason they were always much older than me. And ugly too. I shuddered. It was extraordinary how they seemed convinced that I would say yes. Just because I was on my own. Though of course, once Mario had come along, they had soon kept their distance.

★★★

Half a wall and several dozen jingles later, after doing my best to rinse the worst of the whitewash off my face, arms and legs, I walked the 500 yards up to the village shop to see Tito and pay for the gas bottle. I had nearly reached the top of the steps that led to the glass door when I heard a blood curdling sound coming from somewhere below. A pig was running through the piazza, a terrified look in its eyes. Behind it, in hot pursuit, were Giovanni and Luca, followed by their father Benedetto, all three of them brandishing knives. I looked away and quickly opened the shop door. A couple of women were there buying tinned tomatoes and pasta, chatting in a conspiratorial way. It was impossible to hear what they were saying over the sound of the pig's desperate squealing, which was now becoming even louder. The women nodded to me and stepped aside so that I could be served. They were clearly not in any hurry.

"Ah, *buongiorno Signorina*. What a pleasure to see you again. Now I can give you your change." Tito appeared to be in an uncommonly good mood. I handed him the 25,000 lire note.

"Now that you have something to cook on, maybe I can interest you in some pasta. You could make a nice sauce with a little garlic and tinned tomatoes. Even if you are on your own, you should always eat properly. How about *spaghetti al tonno* this evening?" It sounded like a good idea and I bought some tinned tuna, canned tomatoes and pasta. I turned down the offer of this morning's already stale-looking bread.

"If that will be all *Signorina*, let me wish you a very pleasant afternoon," said Tito cheerfully. "Come on ladies, it's five to one and I'm closing in a few minutes. I have an important phone call to make."

"Looks like Benedetto and his family will be eating well this Easter," said one of the women, looking in the direction from which the pig's squealing had been coming. The noise had gone quiet now, so I calculated it would be safe to leave the shop.

Descending the steep steps, I noticed Generosa washing clothes at the village fountain a few feet away. She called me over.

"Ciao *Stellina*", she beamed, wiping her wet soapy hands on her pinafore and smothering me with her ample bosom. Though her hair was now snow white, it was not hard to see that Generosa had once been a very good looking woman. She still had large brown eyes and full red lips and swayed her now broad hips coquettishly as she moved around the fountain.

"I want you to explain. Why is it that all English men wear skirts? They may dress like girls, but I can tell you, they're real men all right!" She broke off into a raucous laugh, wiping a tear from the corner of one eye.

It took me a while to work out what she was talking about, but then I remembered something I had heard when I first arrived. Generosa had been a rare beauty when she was younger and had given a warm welcome to some of the Scottish regiment that had passed through this part of Umbria during the Second World War after landing at Anzio. She certainly hadn't forgotten them.

A short distance away from her, also doing the family laundry, was Settima. It was clear that the two women did not get on. They worked with their arms wet up to their elbows, side by side, but back to back.

Just then, a car drove up into the piazza. Two policemen headed towards us and started talking to Generosa. They wanted to know about some pots and pans they thought she might have taken.

"You lot in San Massano are just a bunch of thieves," said the younger police officer. He helped his colleague bundle the loudly protesting Generosa into the back of their car.

"Don't take any notice. That policeman is from Montebello, and they have always had it in for us," said Settima to me, watching the car drive off. Her expression was one of smug satisfaction. I asked her why they had taken Generosa and what would happen now.

"She shouldn't have taken what really belonged to me. I hope they put her in prison," said Settima.

"My husband realised he had been too hasty, and when he went down with you to Montebello the other day, he told the police just what Generosa had done." Settima went back to her work, singing one of the songs I had heard on the radio that afternoon. As I turned to leave my glance fell, to my horror, on the sight of the pig, now quiet and still, strung up from a hook in the corner as Benedetto and his sons worked swiftly on its carcass with their knives.

I had been living in the village for quite a few weeks before I learned to my surprise that I was not the only foreigner in the area. Apart from Angela of course, who, as her husband often said, didn't really count. He had a point. Angela had been immersed in Italian life for so many years now that she had started to make mistakes in English. She was always talking about how she was going to control the pasta instead of check how it was doing and saying how delicious the spaghetti were. And how Ercolino should brush his hairs. The irony that she made a small income giving English lessons to children down in Terni was not entirely lost on her.

"I don't know which language I'm speaking most of the time," she said. She was clearing up after giving Mamma her weekly shower in her small flat in Terni. I had dropped by after driving down to pick up some more whitewash. "Luckily, they don't seem to notice."

One morning, Generosa, now back home after a stern warning from the Montebello police, stopped me to break the news that George and the *Colonello* were due back that day. George, or *Giorgio* as she called him, was an American actor who lived most of the time in Rome and had a house in San Massano.

"Giorgio is a wonderful man. You are certain to like him,"

said Generosa. "You know, he's sometimes on the television!" I looked forward to the prospect of seeing a new face, especially someone who spoke the same language. Although everyone was friendly in this busy Italian community, it could sometimes get quite lonely.

I wasn't disappointed. George was great company, with an almost non-stop barrage of irreverent jokes and stories, many of them drawn from his strange life on a Rome cinema set where he appeared in weekly episodes of a popular TV detective series. Big and burly, with blond hair and a beard, the American was always on some faddish diet, which he would forget about instantly when one of the village women placed a large plate of pasta in front of him.

With him was the *Colonello*, a retired colonel from the US airforce who went wherever George did, and clearly worshipped him. George told me the Colonel's story as we sat out on his terrace later that evening over a glass of chilled vodka. Bizarrely, there was a toilet set on a high plinth right in the middle of the bedroom that led out onto the terrace. I would make sure that I never needed to use that, I resolved to myself.

"I drink vodka these days. Wine's too fattening," said George. He helped himself to a large slice of pecorino cheese, part of a cheese-only diet that he had read about in a magazine and was currently pursuing. The Colonel had been a pilot in the allied bombing raids that had devastated Terni during the war.

"He never forgave himself," said George, cutting off another chunk of cheese from a slab of gorgonzola. "So he always said he would come back to this area to live one day." The Colonel, whose family owned a big pharmaceuticals company, kept his promise and struck up a friendship with George whom he met one day in Terni. Over the years, the former pilot had become old and infirm and George had become his carer, paid a substantial sum for the job by the Colonel's grown up sons, who hardly ever saw their father. In spite of the fact that the old man was now in a wheelchair, George took him everywhere he went, much to the displeasure of his string of female companions. His latest girlfriend was from Sweden, and they planned to get married at Christmas.

"It's time I settled down, and Asa is a lovely girl," said George. He finished his second vodka and stood up. "Come on, we'd better go and see what he's up to with Generosa. I bet he's giving her English lessons."

Because of the difficulty of getting the wheelchair up the steep slope into the narrow alleyway where his house was, George had rigged up a camper van in the piazza and installed the Colonel in it. When they were in San Massano, Generosa was paid to wash, feed and keep an eye on the former pilot, who spent most of his time watching movies at full volume about General Patton, and trying to teach Generosa the rudest words he could think of in the English language.

"Keeess ma hass," came the halting refrain from inside the camper as we walked down the slope.

"No, No. There's no aitch in ass. Try again. *Ancora!*"

"Keeess ma hass ancora!"

"You're never going to teach her that Pops," said George, giving a pat on the back to the white-haired old man. "Maybe you should try something ruder. By the way, I've brought someone to meet you. She's from England."

"How do you do Ma'am?" the Colonel was suddenly a gentleman again and held out a frail hand.

"Hey, that's not a bad idea George. I'll try to think of something different to teach her. Something really rude."

It was George who, inadvertently, solved the mystery of something that had been puzzling me for some time now. I had spent hours clearing brambles and weeds to turn a small corner of my garden into a vegetable plot. But though the seedlings I planted and watered carefully each day blossomed into sturdy plants, I never managed to harvest a single courgette, aubergine or tomato. Every time I thought the vegetables might be ready for picking, I arrived to find cut-off stems.

"I'm sure Generosa is stitching me up, but it keeps the Colonel happy," said George as we walked back from the camper. "You know what they say here. *Scarpe grosse, cervello fino.*"

Actually I didn't. That was another phrase they had never taught me at Cambridge. I translated it out loud: "Big shoes, fine brains. What was that supposed to mean?"

"It's a saying about peasants here in Italy. And it means that though they may wear hob-nailed boots, they are very sharp people. Even the women. Especially the women. By the way, I saw Settima walking back from your place early this morning with a big armful of vegetables. Don't worry. It's nothing personal. I know for a fact that when I'm away she hooks her electricity up to mine."

The sun was getting hot now, and although up here in the hills there was always a faint breeze, it was becoming too warm to contemplate doing anything at all. The relentless chorus of the cicadas was beginning to make me feel drowsy. I said goodbye to George and headed back down the hill towards my house. The thought of a siesta in my back garden was very appealing.

"Don't forget I'm having a party in the piazza on Saturday," George called after me. "It's my last night here for a while and I'm inviting the whole village. There'll be a few people from other places as well. I hope you'll come."

I called back that I would. I headed for home, running through the items in my very small wardrobe. It would be fun to go to a party.

I was suddenly very tired, and sitting down against the stump of an old olive tree near the vegetable patch, I closed my eyes. The chorus of cicadas had become intense, working its way up to an almost deafening crescendo. It can't have been more than a few minutes later that I awoke with a start, alerted by a strange sense of unease and a slow rustling that seemed to be coming from close by. My glance fell on a coiled brown shape, which was unravelling itself slowly, just a few inches from my bare feet. I leapt up, my heart beating furiously as the snake darted off into the undergrowth.

That had been a very close call. I knew from the drawings I had seen on a noticeboard down in Montebello that this was a viper. If you got bitten by one of those, you had about twenty minutes to live. The official advice was to stay calm to prevent the poison from spreading more rapidly through the bloodstream. All very well when the nearest hospital was twenty-five minutes away. I ran into the house and closed all the shutters, shaking. It took a lot to scare me, but I hated snakes. What on earth had possessed me to buy a house in a place where they were so common?

When the shaking subsided, and I calculated that the shops would have reopened after the long siesta, I drove down to Montebello to the pharmacy. It was run by a charming old man who had been to summer school at Magdalene College, Oxford in his youth, and liked nothing better than to speak a bit of English and reminisce about what he described as his 'appiest days. It would not be a quick visit, but he would almost certainly know what to do.

A good half hour later I emerged from his store, clutching a bag with a box containing a rubber tourniquet with a picture on the outside of a brown snake with black markings. There was also a small plastic suction device to remove the poison in the event of a bite, and another box containing a small phial of snake serum, together with a large syringe.

"If you are bitten on the leg, then you have to inject the serum into your thigh," said the voluble pharmacist.

"If it bites you on the hand or arm, then you must inject it into your shoulder."

He had plenty of other helpful advice.

"Make a lot of noise when you go out in the garden. That scares them off. Or you could keep some turkeys. They're very good at pecking off snakes' heads."

I was beginning to feel queasy again at the thought of it, and made for the door.

"But don't forget," he said as I turned to say goodbye. "You must keep the serum in the refrigerator."

A fridge. I still didn't have one. How was I going to keep my snake serum cool, and for that matter, how was I going to survive the rest of the summer without one? I was pondering my dilemma when a voice called out from across the road.

"Good evening *Signorina*. May I offer you a drink?"

It was Agostino, Natalino's uncle. A tall, solid looking man who had spent his life in the fields and had never married, he was seated at the bar owned by Elisa and her husband Valerio, who also lived in San Massano. When the bar closed, at ten o'clock, he would get a lift back up the hill with them in their little white Fiat Panda. Until then, he would sip a generous measure of vermouth and watch the world go by, as he did most evenings.

Unlike his sister Grazia, who always appeared to be cross, Agostino had one of those faces that never seemed to stop smiling.

"Sit down and have a rest. You look pale," he said kindly, pulling out a chair for me. I accepted and ordered a Martini to keep him company.

"Could I please have some ice in it?" I asked Elisa, who had come to the table to see who Agostino was talking to. She kissed me on both cheeks when she saw who it was, but she was sorry, she couldn't give me any ice.

"The Martini is cold. It's kept in the cooler. You can't have ice in your drink when it's this hot," she said, with a slight expression of exasperation. "It's terribly bad for you."

Agostino muttered something to Elisa as she left and turned back to ask me what the matter was. I explained about my encounter with the snake.

"Well the best thing you can do is burn some old shoes or tyres in the garden", he said. "They hate the smell, you know. "And another thing, always wear thick trousers. They've saved my life on more than one occasion." A closer look at Agostino revealed that, in spite of the heat, he was wearing thick brown moleskin trousers and a long-sleeved flannel shirt.

He went on to recount the last time a viper bit him as he tended the vines a few hundred yards from his house. From the way he talked, it sounded like a fairly regular occurrence.

"The *bestiaccia* – the little beast — couldn't get through the fabric, so although it left a mark with its fangs, the venom didn't get into my blood," he said. He took another sip from his drink at the memory. "Otherwise I wouldn't be here now. You have to be very careful, you know. The worst time is in the spring, when they have their young."

The conversation turned to snake serum, and my problem with keeping it cool. As if on cue, Elisa emerged and, winking at Agostino, popped the smallest blob of ice I had ever seen into my drink.

"There now, that shouldn't do you too much harm," she said. She whisked the rest of the tiny ice cube tray away with her.

Agostino had an idea. He had quite a good fridge in his cellar that he never really used. He ate most of his meals with his sister's family anyway. He would send it up with Natalino the following morning.

The fridge duly arrived on the back of the family's small tractor-driven trailer. Although not tall, Natalino was strong and he hauled it up the stone steps and plugged it into the kitchen wall. I had press tickets for a concert that was being staged that evening to announce the programme for the Festival of the Two Worlds in Spoleto which would be held in the summer. I had managed to get a commission from a well known magazine in London to write a piece about the thriving arts festival that was beginning to make a name for this pretty little hill town, and if all went well, I might be able to sell it to some of the newspapers in America and Australia that I had contacted.

"Natalino, how about coming with me to a concert this evening in Spoleto?" It seemed the least I could do to repay him for his help. Natalino was enthusiastic. He loved Spoleto, though he had only been there once for an ice cream. It was so different from San Massano, he said, watching me transfer my precious snake serum into my new fridge, which had started to whirr. With all those bars, and restaurants and people milling about.

Aside from a couple of stifled yawns, Natalino put up a good performance that evening, though you could see that Mozart's Magic Flute, in German, was not particularly to his taste.

"To tell you the truth, I prefer Vasco Rossi," he said shyly. "And I couldn't always work out what was going on. Let's go for an ice cream. I'll take you to the bar I went to last time I came here."

He was right about Spoleto, which was quite the prettiest town I had seen so far. Across from the small Renaissance theatre was a 13th century cathedral built in a pale coloured stone which caught the last of the sun's rays as swallows swooped and dived under its porticoes. Around the corner, narrow cobbled streets full of shops and *trattorias* led off from a main piazza, with a Roman arch at one end and a marble fountain at the other. All around the square, there were pastel-coloured houses with flowers cascading from Juliet balconies. Next to the bar where we sat to have our ice cream, a stringed quartet was playing a medley of Vivaldi. I would have to stay up a good part of the night to write my article, but it had been worth it.

Next morning, as soon as I knew the shop would be open, I walked up to Tito's with my Tandy in hand. I had paid more than a month's salary shortly before leaving England for what the salesman in Fleet Street had assured me was the latest breakthrough in computer technology. The laptop had such a small memory that it could only hold one article at a time, so you had to wipe the first one off before you could write another. But it could send stories straight down the wire, and seemed like the answer to all my problems.

Tito's telephone booth had a metre that clocked up the cost of the calls anyone made. I walked in with the Tandy under my arm, and he eyed the contraption suspiciously. The shopkeeper paused to ask me how my love life was going. Was I any closer to finding a husband?

Dodging the question I had come to dread, I closed the door to the hot and stuffy cubicle at the back of the shop. With sweat pouring down my face from the heat and the effort, I desperately tried to ram the handset into the acoustic coupler that came with the kit. As I soon discovered, getting a connection was more miss than hit and it took a good hour before my story was winging its way down the line.

Tito, who had been hovering outside the door, was mystified.

"What have you been doing all this time?" he said. "I didn't hear you speaking."

He looked at the metre for the hundredth time, and tried to work out why it hadn't moved. He knew I had been calling England, America and Australia, but it was too complicated to explain about reverse charge calls.

"Are you sure I'm not going to get a huge bill for this?" he asked me doubtfully. "I have a sister in Adelaide, and when I call her at Christmas it costs me a fortune." I resolved to hold an imaginary conversation out loud next time I had to send a story. This first time, the whole business had taken the best part of a morning as Tito insisted I have a glass of *Viparo*, a vile local herb liqueur, and venture into the shop itself to inspect his wares again. "You might as well stock up now for anything you might need in the next day or two," he said. "I'll be driving to fetch Clara on Thursday. She's going to spend the day here planning some of the changes she wants to make to her new home. So I won't be opening the shop for a couple of days. It's the first time I've ever closed since I first started the shop twenty five years ago."

A rusty orange Fiat parked at the bottom of the drive alerted me to the visitors several minutes before I saw them. It had a Terni number plate and two of its tyres were almost completely bald. I walked up the slope and saw two men prowling around the front of my house, peering in through the windows and inspecting the stonework.

"*Buongiorno*. Can I help you?"

They both swung round abruptly at the sound of my voice. They must be related, maybe father and son. Both of them had the same straggly dark orange hair and small shifty eyes and both had lighted cigarettes in their hands. The older man stared for several seconds before breaking into a thin smile. Several of his teeth were missing, and the others were badly stained.

"You must be the English woman who has come to live here."

There was something in his manner that was decidedly unattractive.

"I see you like growing vegetables *Signorina*."

He jabbed his cigarette in the direction of my small vegetable plot. A quick glance revealed that there were two fewer spring cabbages than there had been when I left earlier that morning.

I told him that I did and asked him who he was and what I could do for him. There was another wall to be painted and I was anxious to make a start on it.

"Settimio's the name, and this is my son, Ernesto. My father used to live in part of this house you've just bought. He died last November, bless his soul."

He paused to light another cigarette, passing one to his son who stood next to him, an expression of ugly defiance on his face.

"We'd like to have a little talk with you about business. You see, that vegetable plot is our land. We'll sell it to you if you like."

"It can't possibly be your land. It's right outside my house."

"Sorry lady. But you're wrong. It's ours." He thrust a sheaf of papers under my nose. "See, this is the map from the land register office in Terni. I went there this morning. This piece of land is ours, and so is all this strip of land running right the way around your house."

He pointed a nicotine stained finger with bitten nails at the map, showing a shaded area that appeared to circle the entire house.

"We don't want to be greedy, so we'll make you a reasonable offer. If you give us five million lire, we'll say no more about it, and you can go on planting your vegetables. But if you don't, we can make life very difficult for you." He broke into another smile, and his son smiled too, revealing the same assortment of stained and missing teeth.

"If you don't give us the money, lady, then you won't be able to get in or out of your house. And that won't be very nice will it? So think about it lady. We'll give you a fortnight."

"Yeah, think about it," piped up the son." And with that, they turned on their heels and strode off down the drive.

Chapter Four

Ercolino was in a lyrical mood.

"You see, friends are like the stars. You can't always see them, but they are always there. You've got friends here, and we'll sort it out for you. Don't worry."

But I was very worried. And so, it seemed, was Cesare, who was sitting opposite me at the table in Ercolino's house in Terni. The usually jovial scout master was clearly deeply concerned.

"I know that family and they have always been trouble makers," he said darkly, wringing his huge hands through his thick black hair and tugging at his goatee beard. "Their father was completely different. A delightful man. As long as he was alive it was no problem. But the son is quite another matter. And his son is even worse."

With Tito's shop closed for two days, there was no way of telephoning, so I had driven down to see Ercolino as soon as the two menacing visitors had left. Cesare had been summoned immediately and a council of war assembled. Angela was next door in the kitchen, playing cards with Mamma, who was merciless at her favourite game *Scopa,* and would call out triumphantly every time she won a trick.

"I'll go and see my friend Gianni. He works at the land register office and he'll be able to tell me what's going on," said Cesare. "And then there is Luigi, who's a notary. He should be able to help."

"See what I mean?" said Ercolino, passing a glass of *nocino,* a liqueur made from walnuts, towards Cesare. "Everyone needs friends. Especially in Italy."

"No thank you. I couldn't drink a thing. I'm too angry," said Cesare, pushing the glass away. "I can't believe those good-for-nothings can come and threaten a young girl like that, and someone who is a guest in our country. It makes my blood boil."

"*Scopa!*" A triumphant shout came from next door. Mamma was clearly on a winning streak.

I accepted Ercolino's offer of *nocino* gratefully and downed the small glass in one. The encounter with the two men in San Massano had shaken me and I was beginning to be seriously worried about their threats. Five million lire was a great deal of money, especially at the moment. Where on earth was I going to find it?

"*Scopa!*"

Cesare stood up to go.

"I'd better be off to start making a few calls," he said. "I'll be in touch as soon as I have any news."

I too rose to leave, first popping my head around the kitchen door to say goodbye to Angela and Mamma, who was carefully scanning the cards left in her hand.

"*Scopa!* That's it, I've won!" she yelled, slamming down her winning flush on the formica table.

"You're a wonderful daughter-in-law Angela, but you're no match for me. You know what they say: lucky in love, unlucky in cards."

Angela stood up to give me a kiss.

"Try not to worry too much," she said. "Cesare will sort it out if anyone can. We'll be up to San Massano at the weekend, so we'll see you then."

I slept badly that night, tossing and turning on the stiff horsehair mattress that I hadn't got round to replacing yet. There was still so much to do and buy that it was hard to know where to start. When I finally did get to sleep, my dreams were peppered with toothless faces leering through barred windows, holding up cabbages as they grinned at me. There was a giant padlock on the door so there was no way out.

The next couple of days passed in a blur, with most of it spent painting the kitchen walls. Every so often I looked out of the window uncomfortably to check if the duo had returned. On the third day, my food reserves dangerously low and aching from all the work, I headed for the piazza, where I caught sight of some official-looking notices pinned on one of the walls.

"Municipal elections", they announced, exhorting all good citizens to cast their vote at the polling station, which would be housed at Montebello primary school. The date set was two days hence. As I read, I noticed an unusually smart and shiny car draw up into the piazza. The driver, whom I had seen down at the bar in Montebello, got out and opened the rear door to let out the only passenger, a tall corpulent priest with a ruddy face. This must be Don Gaetano, who lived in Abacone, further up the valley. His parish included all the smaller villages in the neighbourhood, and he took his job seriously, reporting to his boss, the Bishop of Spoleto at their weekly meetings. San Massano was his special cross to bear. The villagers did not always obey God's teachings in the way that they led their daily lives, and not all of them turned up for Mass on Sundays.

Tito, who had followed me down the steps, greeted Don Gaetano respectfully and stepped forward to introduce us.

"This is the most recent citizen to take up residency in San Massano," said the shopkeeper, with a touch of pride. "She doesn't have any parents, and she doesn't have a husband yet, but I am sure that the good Lord will provide." The priest seemed more interested in my religion. Was I a Catholic, and did I have the right to vote in Italy? I told him I was an Anglican, omitting to add that I almost never went to church. And as far as I knew, I had no right to vote. He seemed perplexed.

"An Anglican. Does that mean you are not a Christian like

73

us?" The conversation was interrupted as Don Gaetano noticed his driver setting up what appeared to be a blackboard in the corner of the piazza.

"Not there you fool. Put it in the middle, where everyone can see it properly," thundered the priest. "Now get some chairs, and make sure everyone knows they have to be here in the piazza. Ring the church bells if necessary. Buy some food from the shop. Anything to get them out. I want them all here at ten o'clock sharp."

Tito helped the driver fetch some old chairs from the cellar beneath his shop. The pair of them arranged the seating like a cinema, before climbing the stairs to the shop. The driver emerged a few minutes later, with a tray full of cheese, *capocollo* – a cured meat not unlike prosciutto — and slices of *pizza al formaggio*, a savoury cake made with local sheep's cheese. Tito followed close behind with some plastic cups and a bottle of *Viparo*. He coughed as he looked at the priest.

"Don Gaetano, I don't wish to dwell on such a trifling matter at a time like this, but the bill for all the food and drink comes to 54,000 lire."

Fumbling under his surplice, Don Gaetano drew out a small black leather purse and counted out the money carefully into Tito's outstretched palm. Meanwhile, the villagers had begun filtering into the piazza, drawn by the clanging of the church bells, but also by the promise of something to eat and drink. What was Don Gaetano up to? He was usually such a gruff character, haranguing his parishioners from the pulpit and lecturing them on the error of their ways.

The priest had taken up his position in front of the blackboard, which was now strategically placed in front of the villagers.

"*Buongiorno* everyone, and welcome to this little impromptu gathering," he said, with a fixed smile on his face.

"First of all, I want to explain something very important to

74

you. So please pay attention. Then afterwards you can eat and drink." Slowly, and choosing his words with what appeared to be great care, the priest explained to the now packed piazza that in two days' time, they would be expected to make some important choices.

"Now I know that some of you will find it confusing, and I am well aware that there are some people in our midst who have difficulties remembering some of the basic lessons they learned at school," he said, looking in the direction of Benedetto, Caterina and Settima. "That is why I have come here today, to help you understand what you must do."

"I'll vote for anyone who can save my poor Fabrizio from doing his military service," came a voice from the back. It was Colomba, who was beside herself with worry at the prospect of having to see her son go into the army for a year. He had just turned eighteen, and the call up was bound to come soon.

The priest ignored the comment and turned to the blackboard. On it, he had drawn a large square, divided up into two halves. On one side there was the symbol of the DC – the *Partito Democratico Cristiano*. Next to it, he had placed a big tick. On the other side of the square was the hammer and sickle of the PCI – the *Partito Comunista Italiano*.

"Whatever you do, do not put your cross here," said Don Gaetano. "These people are the scum of the earth and will bring ruin to you and your families. If you put your cross here, you will face the wrath of God and the Holy Father, and you will be excommunicated from the Church."

Reaching for one of the napkins brought down by Tito, he rubbed out the hammer and sickle in disgust.

"Make sure you put your cross here, where you see this picture, he said, pointing to the DC's logo of a red and white shield. "And remember, there will be a free bus service down to the polling station at Montebello and back again later.

Afterwards, the Bishop has instructed me to offer a free hamper to every family who does their duty."

It was time for me to get back to my decorating, so leaving the villagers to their unexpected mid-morning feast, I headed down the road to my house. With the kitchen walls now finished, the next job would be staining the beams. Using my now tried and tested system of piling a chair on top of the kitchen table to reach the ceiling, I dipped my brush into the brown liquid in the plastic mineral water bottle that I had cut in half to use as a container. I had wrapped an old silk scarf around my hair and put my ski goggles on again, with plastic yellow gloves to protect my hands. But no matter how careful I was, the walnut solution trickled down my bare arms and into the gloves, leaving a dark snail-like trail. When I climbed down for a break half an hour later, I saw from my pocket mirror that I had also managed to get a spattering over my forehead and on one of my cheeks. This stuff took ages to get rid of and it was George's party that evening. A painful session in the bathroom with soap and a scrubbing brush lay ahead of me.

Hopefully George's party would go better than the one I had thrown a couple of weeks after my arrival. I had brought some bottles of Pimms over in my suitcase from England, thinking it would make a refreshing drink. There was also white wine, lemonade for the children and some packets of peanuts and crisps, though they only seemed to sell plain ones in the shops around here. I had told everyone to come at six-thirty pm, expecting them to arrive about half an hour later, but they turned up on the dot, the whole village marching in force up the drive. I ushered them onto the terrace that Benedetto had built, and started handing out drinks.

"Oh no thank you. I'm *astemia*," said Colomba, as I offered her a glass. "I'll just take a glass of water for the time being."

Most of the other women said the same, and I soon worked out that almost all the women were teetotal. They did, however, devour the peanuts and the crisps, looking around expectantly for something else and as I milled between the various groups with my jugs of wine and Pimms, I began to have an uneasy feeling.

"I've already had one," said Amato, Colomba's husband, when I went to fill up his glass. "I can't have another one until I've eaten." Only Pompeo accepted a refill, his eyes taking on a watery glaze as he downed his fourth glass of wine. Mirella, standing next to Cesare who had dressed in his scout's uniform for the occasion, drew me aside.

"When are you serving the food?" she whispered. "I think everyone is hungry and if you don't bring it out soon, Pompeo will be falling over." I struggled to explain that I had no food. This was supposed to be a drinks party.

It was Ercolino who saved the day, disappearing suddenly and returning ten minutes later, his arms piled high with parcels wrapped in greaseproof paper. He had been down to the *rosticceria* in Lavena, and had bought a selection of fried courgette flowers, artichokes and aubergines in olive oil, as well as tomatoes stuffed with rice and herbs. Another parcel contained pieces of grilled chicken with potatoes, cut into cubes and roasted with sprigs of rosemary.

"You English people always think about drinking, but here in Italy, we think more about eating," said Ercolino, as Angela helped me serve the food on some plates I had brought out from the kitchen.

For his party, George had wisely put all the arrangements in the hands of Generosa, and the tables set out in the piazza were laden with food, all of it cooked by the village women who had now changed out of their overalls and into their best dresses.

"I'll just pick up the bill at the end of it," said George,

pouring me a glass of white wine from a five-litre flagon. He was drinking Campari.

"It has fewer calories you know."

Ignoring my look of disbelief, he took my arm and steered me towards a long table.

"Come and meet some people."

Some of the guests were people I already knew. The Colonel was sitting in his wheelchair at the head of the table, and on seeing me he reached for my hand and kissed it with an air of gallantry.

"So glad you could come Ma'am," he said. "Try some of the pasta. It's very good." Generosa, seated next to him, leapt up and threw her arms around me. Her effusive greetings still caught me slightly off balance, but it was impossible not to be captivated by her roguish charm.

"*Stella mia*, did you know you have truffles on the land outside your house? I can show you where they are and we can share what we find." She took a step closer so that her huge bosoms were pressed against me.

"But don't tell Settima," she whispered urgently. "She's not to be trusted."

Smiling broadly at the scene he had just witnessed was a young man in his mid-twenties seated a few places down the table. His chestnut-coloured hair fell over olive-green eyes, and his well-shaped teeth flashed when he grinned.

"This is Mario," said George, moving to introduce us. "He's a friend of mine who's come to be here with us tonight, all the way from Naples."

That explained it. He didn't look as if he came from around here, and I knew I hadn't seen him before.

"And this is Mario's girlfriend Laura." The girlfriend was heavily made up with a cigarette in one hand and a slightly sulky expression.

"Pleased to meet you." She shook my hand limply. Then turning to Mario she said:

"I don't want to be boring, but can we go home soon? We've got a very long drive back."

Laura got up to go to the bathroom, and Mario beckoned me to sit down beside him. We started chatting and I asked him about life in Naples, a place that had always held a strange fascination, though I had only been there once some years before.

"Is it true what you hear about the *Camorra*," I asked. "Does it really have such a hold on the city?"

"Oh yes," he replied, pouring a glass of wine for me and one for himself, and passing me a plate of artichoke hearts. "My aunt runs a small boutique, and she often receives a visit from a local character, asking for what he calls a contribution. It's protection money, of course. Once, when she forgot to pay it, she had another visit from a couple of thugs who held a gun to her head until she got the money from the till. But there's a great deal more to Naples than the *Camorra*. It's a beautiful place, in a decadent run-down kind of way."

As we talked on, a small band struck up in the corner of the piazza, led by an accordion playing a medley of popular Italian songs. Ercolino and Angela, who had arrived in the village earlier that day, stood up to dance, Ercolino twirling his wife around at a dizzying pace. Looking at his feet, I noticed he was wearing a fetching pair of green leather moccasins with dark green tassels. Following their lead, other couples took to the floor: Generosa and her tiny husband Fiorello and even Settima and Pompeo, though Pompeo was swaying dangerously, and not always in time to the music. Colomba was ruffling the hair of her son Fabrizio fondly, a gesture he ducked every now and then. He appeared to be more interested in the girl in front of him, who was standing quietly at the side of her sister and her parents. This was Melissa, whose light brown hair fell halfway down her back and whose large almond-shaped eyes were a rich shade of hazel. Her father, Vitale, hardly ever let her out, so this evening had been a rare treat. Tito was by himself, seated at the edge of the dance floor thinking wistfully of Clara, whom he had driven back to her own village after showing her around San Massano and introducing her to his father. The old man was sitting nearby, surveying the scene with a contented expression on his frail face, exchanging the occasional comment with Natalino's grandfather, who was sitting next to him.

Vast quantities of food continued to be passed around the long table: homemade pizza filled with fresh greens picked from the hillsides by the village women, long metal dishes of *lasagne*, bowls of pasta with wild asparagus, casseroles of rabbit cooked in white wine, platters of sausages and tiny lamb chops grilled on an open barbecue and huge dishes of *zuppa inglese*, the Italian name for trifle. Big terracotta jugs of local red and white wine were gradually being emptied, but as soon as the last drop was gone, a fresh one would appear to take its place.

"What a wonderful evening. It has been a great pleasure meeting you." Mario, who was sipping a second cup of espresso, said this last bit in English, surprisingly good English in a country where most people spoke it badly or not at all. I asked him where he had learned it.

"Oh I work for a big English company," he said. "And now I'm afraid it looks as if my time is up. A pity as I was rather enjoying myself." He looked in the direction of Laura who was making her way back to the table after saying her goodbyes. She had an impatient look on her face.

"Perhaps we'll meet up again. George is a good friend of mine, so I hope so."

I would soon have to leave too. The next day, I had more beams to paint and it was time I got down to writing some articles to make some money. The figure of five million lire kept creeping into my thoughts, and there was less than a week to go.

By Tuesday morning the kitchen ceiling was at last finished, and although my hands and arms were now almost indelibly streaked with walnut stain, the room was beginning to take shape. There were still no cupboards, though the flatpacks of some kitchen units that I had found in Terni were stacked up against one wall, waiting to be assembled. And there were no tiles on the floor which was still ugly grey concrete. Still, there was my new cooker in one corner, which I had only used once, and Agostino's fridge purring away comfortingly in another. Perhaps it was time to start filling it with some real food. I felt guilty not going to Tito's, but he didn't have much apart from canned tuna and tomatoes and what little he had seemed to cost twice the price of anywhere else. In between my back-breaking sessions with the walnut solution I had got out my typewriter and dashed off several letters to newspapers in England, Canada and the USA suggesting story ideas from Italy. It was time to take a trip out into the big wide world and get them posted. There was still no word from Cesare.

Lavena was a three kilometre drive down the winding lanes that passed through gnarled chestnut trees and round the side of the hill that rose up imposingly from the valley in front of my house. Newborn lambs were grazing next to their mothers in the fields and cows and calves of a startling white colour were moving out of an old brick barn and strolling into the long grass. Its small sunroof open, my little *Cinquecento* flew round the curves, hugging them perfectly. Ercolino had been right. It was the ideal car for these roads.

Further down the hill, the chestnut groves gave way to olive trees and a large round stone marked the entrance to the mill where local farmers took their harvests to be made into oil. Natalino had told me that he always slept the night there, when he drove his tractor and trailer down in November with the dozen or so bags of olives he and his family picked from the trees they owned on the slopes beneath San Massano.

"It gets cold at night, but it's worth it," he had said. "You can never be too sure. I like to see my olives going into the mill and watching them come out as oil the other end. That way I know they are not palming me off with someone else's, or trying to cheat me on the amount of oil I get back."

Finding somewhere to park was never easy in Lavena, for although it was not much bigger than San Massano, with just one road running through it, everyone seemed to have some sort of a vehicle, including an old man who had been crippled from birth and who drove around the village all day long in a home-made contraption that was half motorbike and half tractor trailer, stopping to talk to anyone he met on the way. But this morning I was in luck, as a young man was just pulling out, and with a sharp blow of the whistle that he kept on a chain fastened to his shirt pocket, the local policeman ushered me in to the empty space, and gallantly opened the door to let me out.

"*Buongiorno Signorina*. Have you come to get your newspaper?"

How was it that everyone around here knew exactly who I was and what I was doing almost before I did?

"*Buongiorno*," I replied. "Yes, I've come for a newspaper and a few supplies."

"You'll find the best food is sold in the shop next to the bar," said the policeman, twirling his prolific handlebar moustache. "It's run by my two sisters and they have everything you could possibly need. You should try the prosciutto. It comes from our own pigs."

Thanking him and moving first to the tiny newspaper shop, I glanced at the billboard for the local daily, propped outside.

"*Pensionato schiacciato da un trattore*" read the headline. A pensioner had been crushed by a tractor about fifteen kilometres from here, and his whole village was in mourning, the billboard announced.

"*Buongiorno Signorina.* The usual? A neatly folded copy of the *Corriere della Sera* was already waiting for me on the counter. The white-haired man who ran the store heaved himself up slowly from his chair and moved to hold out a bony hand to shake mine.

"I saw you drive past and I knew you'd come and get your paper," he said. I don't get much call for the *Corriere della Sera* around here, but I always keep one for you. How is the house going?"

The newspaper shop owner must have been at least eighty and it was hard to see how he could make much of a living in his tiny shop where the light barely penetrated. It sold everything from plastic combs to buttons, all kept in a bewildering array of boxes stacked high on the shelves. Nothing cost more than a few hundred lire, but the owner was unfailingly courteous to everyone who came into the store, moving unerringly to the right box every time and putting the notes and coins they gave him in a wooden drawer under the counter before lowering himself back on to his straw covered chair and surveying the comings and goings of the village where he had been born and had spent all his long life.

The next stop was the grocery store. There were two in Lavena, and following the policeman's advice I headed towards the one next to the bar. Inside, eight or nine people were standing at the counter ready to pay for their purchases and ordering slices of cheese and salame from the delicatessen cabinet.

"Oh, the ricotta looks good today. I'll try a couple of *etti* of that" said one middle-aged woman whose arms were full of the items she had picked up on her way through the narrow aisle of the crammed store.

"And give me an *etto* of *pancetta* too. My son loves that in his *carbonara.*"

"And maybe I'd better have a bit of pecorino too. An *etto* will do fine. I can always come back tomorrow."

With each new order, the lady behind the counter patiently lugged a round of cheese or slab of cured meat from under the glass cabinet and, sharpening her long knife, proceeded to cut off some slices, absent-mindedly popping the smaller crumbs and pieces into her own mouth. Her sister, who was manning the till a few feet away, calmly chatted to the other women in the line until the customer was at last ready to pay. Everyone seemed to buy the smallest quantities, coming back the next day to repeat the whole process. The lady paying for her groceries had just one stick of celery, broken off from the rest of the stems, two carrots, four tomatoes, three eggs, wrapped individually in newspaper, and a handful of freshly grated parmesan cheese, which the delicatessen sister poured into a cone of greaseproof paper before deftly twisting the top to make a seal. The other sister painstakingly weighed each purchase on some old brass scales before ringing up the price on a black cast iron till. It was just as well no one ever seemed to be in a hurry around here.

My turn came at last and I ordered some of the home-reared prosciutto recommended by the policeman. Nibbling as she sliced, the delicatessen sister asked if my fridge was working well.

"Very well thank you." How did she know?

I wanted to invite Angela and Ercolino to dinner to repay them for some of their kindness and had decided to roast a chicken. The sister went into the back room and came back with one, a yellow-skinned bird complete with head and legs. She placed it on the scales before wrapping it up in brown paper. Trying not to think about the surgical operation that awaited me I ordered the other things I would need: some olive oil – decanted from a large drum – some salt – sold loose and poured into a paper twist – some pepper – poured into a smaller paper twist – potatoes and tomatoes, all chosen one by one. I hoped that Settima might leave me at least one lettuce from my vegetable plot. To finish, I opted for a selection of local cheeses and a *crostata*, a kind of open tart made with home-made cherry jam.

"How many *etti* of this cheese would you like?"

Etti, which I now knew to be the equivalent of one hundred grams, were quite beyond me. I never knew how much to order. And I had noticed that whatever quantity I asked for, I always got at least half as much again.

"Oh, a couple will do fine," I said casually.

"Here we are. It's a bit over. Three and a half *etti*," said the sister, putting a few crumbled pieces of cheese into her mouth.

Looking at my watch as I emerged with two full carrier bags, I saw that the whole episode had taken an hour and a half. The friendly policeman was chatting to the old crippled man, and seeing my load, he strode over and offered to help.

"I told you it was a good shop. You won't find better produce than what my sisters sell here." He carried my bags towards the car.

"Oh, I wouldn't bother locking it around here," he said. I was searching in my handbag to find my car keys and open the door. "I'm always here to keep an eye on things and in any case, nothing goes missing in this village. Everyone knows everyone else."

By now I was in the driver's seat and had put the keys in the ignition. I turned the key and pulled the starter button. The engine groaned and turned over slowly, then died. I tried again. This time it barely turned over at all.

"That doesn't sound too good. You're never going to make it home at that rate." The policeman peered in through the window.

"Why don't you put it into neutral and coast down to the garage at the bottom of the hill?" He whipped out his whistle, and, blowing it sharply, summoned two teenage boys who had been sitting on mopeds and listening to a transistor radio that one of them held in his hand.

"Instead of wasting time doing nothing, come over here and give the *signorina* a push," ordered the policeman.

"You can't miss it. It's right in front of you as you go down the hill," he said, leaning in through the window again. "His name is Paolo, by the way." The car coasted slowly down the slope, with the help of a shove from the two boys.

The garage was, as the policeman said, conveniently placed at the bottom of the hill, and I pulled the *Cinquecento* to a halt on the forecourt and stepped out. Inside the workshop a pair of boots was sticking out from under an *Ape*.

"Paolo, there's a lady here to see you," said a man who must be the *Ape*'s owner.

"He'll be right with you. He's almost finished."

The mechanic dragged himself out from under the tiny vehicle and stood up to see who wanted him. He had greying hair and glasses, and his face broke into a smile when he saw me. He smeared his dirty hands down his overalls and stretched out a hand.

"*Buongiorno*. What seems to be the trouble *Signorina*?"

I explained that the engine wouldn't start and he moved over to the *Cinquecento*, opening the back to examine the engine and sitting in the driver's seat to turn the key. It made a sad splutter and then died.

"It sounds to me as if you need a new battery," he said. "Let's put a new one in and see if that does the trick. Michele, your *Ape* should be fine now. You can pay me tomorrow. I have to help this *signorina* now."

The *Ape* owner climbed into his vehicle and smiled as it chugged into life.

"See you tomorrow Paolo. *Arivederci Signorina*," he called and swung out onto the forecourt.

"There, that should do it. Let's take it for a test drive and see what happens." Paolo had taken out my old battery and put a new one in its place.

"Jump in," he said. "I haven't seen you before, but you must be the English *signorina* from San Massano."

I climbed into the passenger seat and he turned the key and pressed the starter button. The engine burst into life immediately.

"I thought so, but we'd better make sure." The mechanic put the car into first gear and drove out of the workshop.

"I'll only be a short while," he called out to a middle-aged woman wearing another version of the ubiquitous pinafore, who was tending some flowers near the petrol pumps. "I have to help the *signorina* out with an urgent problem that she has with her car."

It took him less than five minutes to place one of his still grimy hands on my knee, a grip I firmly removed as I asked him to take me back.

"I just thought we could have some fun together," he said, slightly shamefacedly. "You are on your own, after all."

"Can I say it straight out, or do I have to go around the bushes?" Ercolino was sitting at my kitchen table later that evening. Angela was helping to make the salad while I pulled the now headless and footless chicken from the oven and put the potatoes in a bowl, dressing them with olive oil and some fresh mint that grew wild in the garden. The table was covered with a red and white tablecloth that I had bought in Lavena, and with its freshly painted walls and newly stained beams the kitchen looked much better, despite the fact that plates and pots and pans were still piled up in a corner, waiting for the cupboards that had yet to be built. It was the first time I had invited anyone to eat at my house and I was looking forward to the evening, although the episode with the mechanic I now called Dirty Paolo had rather cast a pall over the occasion.

"I'm going to say it straight out. You really must find a boyfriend." I knew Ercolino well enough by now to recognise that he was getting worked up into one of his states. He stood up from the table and started pacing around the room.

"What are you saying Ercolino? That's her business, not yours," said Angela. "Don't take any notice of him. He's always poking his nose into other people's affairs."

"What I'm trying to say is for her own good." Ercolino had pulled out a cigarette now and was waving it emphatically in the air. "She's having all this trouble with the men around here because they see she is on her own, and they think they can take advantage of her. Unfortunately people round here think that if you are a foreign girl you must be an easy touch. If you had a boyfriend, they wouldn't bother you."

"Well there's not much I can do about that, even if I wanted to," I pointed out. "Boyfriends don't exactly grow on trees. And in any case, I'm not sure I want one, at least not at the moment."

"Don't you worry. Someone will turn up just when you least expect it," Angela placed her hands in mine. "Look what happened with me and Ercolino."

It was several days afterwards that the boys from the village appeared on my doorstep to put up my kitchen units for me. Natalino had promised some help and now that he had finished harvesting the hay in the family's field behind the village, and cutting wood for the following winter, he was ready to lend a hand. With him were Fabrizio, Gianmarco from next door, and Felice, who was Pompeo and Settima's son. They had been out catching rabbits, by dazzling them in the glare of the headlights of Gianmarco's car, or rather the car he had borrowed from his father. Gianmarco was Primo's son and had purloined his father's Mercedes to drive up to see his grandmother while his parents were down at their seaside retreat south of Rome.

"He'd kill me if he knew I'd been driving it over the fields," said Gianmarco laughing. "Still, it was worth it. We caught five rabbits. I've left them with my grandmother to be skinned." The boys clearly saw putting up the kitchen units as man's work and wrestled the instruction sheet from my hand as I sat on the floor, putting the first pieces into place. Natalino had bought a large sheet of laminated wood, which he started measuring up for a work surface. With much banter, most of it directed at Fabrizio and his fondness for Melissa, the three worked without a break.

By midnight, the job was finished, and we all stood back to admire the result. The kitchen was transformed.

"Midnight. Time for a *spaghettata*," announced Felice, rummaging in the bag he had brought with him. From it he pulled two giant-sized packs of pasta and some large tins of tomatoes. A *spaghettata*, they explained, was a midnight feast, albeit rather a substantial one. It was a ritual when you had been working hard or out enjoying yourself, especially in the warm summer months. Fabrizio had a reputation for being the biggest eater of all of them, although he was still wiry and athletic.

"I bet you I can eat a kilo of spaghetti," he said. The other two had already placed a large saucepan of water on to boil and started work on the sauce for the pasta. Half an hour later, as we sat down to our plates of *pasta al pomodoro*, accompanied by a flagon of red wine, Fabrizio broke the news that he had received the official letter from the Ministry of Defence. It gave a date in September when he was expected to present himself at the army camp in Viterbo to start his military service. His father had not said a word since the letter had arrived that morning, and his mother had taken to her bed, the sound of stifled sobs coming from her room.

"To be honest, it was a relief to get out this evening," said Fabrizio, who was now on his third plate of pasta. "They didn't make such a fuss when my sister got married and left home last year."

No one relished the thought of doing military service, with those awful haircuts and early morning runs with backpacks, but the others had been more fortunate. Gianmarco's mother, Nadia, had contacts at the ministry and had used them to erase her son's name from the call-up list. Felice, who was a year older, had been pardoned on the grounds that he was the only member of his family bringing in an income, from his job at the olive oil factory on the way to Lavena. This was the truth, for Pompeo had not been able to hold down a job for years and Felice's younger sister Susanna was still at school. No one mentioned Settima's activity on the sidelines. Natalino, who like me was twenty-six, had been granted exemption because of the earthquake that had struck the area eight years earlier, seriously damaging some of the buildings in San Massano and the surrounding villages.

Fabrizio won his bet, demolishing five bowls piled high with pasta, though his pace slowed towards the end.

He held his bowl out for what would be the serving that clinched it. "I might as well make the most of it while I can. I won't eat like this in the army."

When they left, it was almost three o'clock. Felice had just a few hours before he was due to start work at the olive oil depot. Natalino had a busy morning ahead of him stacking the rest of the wood before it got too hot. Gianmarco had to drive his father's car back to the beachside house before his parents woke up and found it missing. And Fabrizio had to try to persuade his mother to come out of the bedroom. As for me, I had more walls to paint.

"*Signoriiiiina. Signoriiiina!* Come quickly!"

I was feeling bleary eyed after my late night and though I was up and dressed in my painting clothes, it took me a while to work out who was calling me. Climbing down from the chair that I was now using to paint the bedroom walls I stuck my head out of the window, forgetting that I was still wearing my ski goggles. Below, staring up in my direction with a puzzled look on his face was Tonino, a small boy from the village. Short for his age and very slight, he looked far younger than his ten years. He had an angelic face, with wide brown eyes, but a foul mouth.

"About ruddy time *Signorina*. I was beginning to give up hope."

"What is it Tonino? Has something happened?"

"Tito sent me down. You're wanted urgently. There's someone on the phone for you."

"Who is it?"

"How should I bloody know? Come quickly. Tito said you'd give me 1000 lire for coming to give you the message."

I grabbed my purse as I flew out of the door, pulling off my goggles and the scarf around my head as I went, though I was still wearing my paint spattered rugby shirt and shorts.

"Here, this is for you," I handed him a crumpled 1000 lire note.

"Thanks *Signorina*. But get a ruddy move on will you?"

Tito was waiting at the top of the steps to his shop when I arrived, breathless, a few minutes later. I hoped it was nothing serious.

"*Buongiorno Signorina*. Quickly, come into the phone cubicle. Your caller has been hanging on for ages. It's Cesare, and he says it's very urgent."

Cesare. He must have some news about the land outside my house.

"*Buongiorno*." Cesare's strong voice came down the line. "I have some news for you. Some good news and some bad news, and I thought you ought to know immediately.

"I think I'll have the good news first please Cesare."

"Well, my friend in the land register office has been looking into the matter of the land around your house and he's come up with some interesting discoveries. It seems that the piece you're using to grow your vegetables does indeed belong to the part of the property that was lived in by the old man until he died. That means you can't use it any more I'm afraid."

"Never mind, someone always came and picked everything I grew anyway. What about the land that runs around the outside of the house?"

91

"That's the good news. My friend took a close look at the plans, and there is no sign at all of anyone else owning that land. It's definitely yours. Which means that those two scoundrels must have forged the copy that they showed you. They probably thought you wouldn't notice."

I breathed a long sigh of relief.

"That's wonderful Cesare. You can't imagine how happy I am to hear that. I've been worried sick about the whole thing. I could never have afforded to pay what they were asking."

"That's why I rang you straight way. You don't have to worry about them anymore. But I'm afraid there's also some not so good news as well, as I said."

"Go on then. Tell me the worst."

"You're not going to like it. But while talking to my friend the notary about this business of land, something else has come to light. It seems that the old man's family has put the part of the property that he lived in up for sale. They're asking quite a lot of money for it, 30 million lire. They've put it in the hands of an estate agent in Terni. And apparently the first potential buyers are coming to look round it this afternoon."

Chapter Five

"Look at the marvellous view that the property commands. On a clear day, you can see the *Cascate delle Marmore* from your kitchen window. They're the highest waterfalls in Europe, you know."

"But there isn't a kitchen. For that matter, there isn't a window either. The glass is missing. You call it a country residence, but it doesn't even have hot and cold running water. Why would anyone want to live in a place like this?" The woman's voice was becoming increasingly petulant.

"Well it may be true that the apartment requires some degree of renovation work." The estate agent hurriedly ushered the couple out of what I knew from my own spying missions to be a series of dark rooms with uneven floors and a musty smell of old mattresses and mice. "But just look at the magnificent grounds. He drew in his breath sharply as he tripped over an ugly pile of empty tinned tomato cans on the patch of grass just outside the main entrance. And he looked incredulously as his gaze fell on Space Bog, which was standing nearby in all its glory, complete with new loo roll propped on the stick lashed to the backrest.

"Listen to the birdsong here. Those are nightingales if I'm not mistaken. You don't hear those down in Terni."

The well dressed estate agent whom I had come to recognise during his frequent visits in recent days could not have given me a better cue if he had wanted to, though from the pained expression on his face as my radio blasted into life, it was quite clear that he had not wanted any such thing. As luck would have it, my bedroom window was directly above the entrance to the part of the property once occupied by the old man and now the object of a discussion between the agent and a youngish Italian couple. This morning I had learned that the pair lived in an apartment with their in-laws in Terni and were anxious to find a place of their own. The husband, dressed in light-coloured trousers with a smart pale green polo shirt, had been following the agent's comments attentively since they arrived ten minutes earlier. He made appreciative remarks every now and then, especially when he was invited to admire the views, which were indeed spectacular. Today, the air was particularly clear and there in the far left corner of a vista that seemed to stretch for ever, was the white foam of the massive waterfalls thundering into the chasm below. The wife, who wore a short-sleeved pale blue dress with matching high-heeled shoes, was clearly less impressed. She was having some difficulty negotiating the uneven ground and became agitated when a bee that had been working diligently on the nearby rosemary bush decide to investigate the newcomers and flew several times around her increasingly red face.

Her husband was now vainly engaged in simultaneously attempting to calm his wife and swat away the insect.

"Get that horrible thing away from me," she shrieked. "You know I am allergic to wasps."

"So how did you get rid of the latest lot?" Angela and I were enjoying a glass of chilled Orvieto from my new fridge. We were in my garden, sitting at a small wrought iron table that Natalino had found for me in the garage of his parents' house. He had found a couple of matching chairs as well.

"I suppose you did the radio trick again?" said Angela, lighting one of the long menthol cigarettes she smoked in summer. "That estate agent must really hate you. Still, your strategy seems to be working."

"Yes, I turned the volume up as loud as possible and tuned into the worst radio station that I could find, one that plays really awful non-stop pop music." I smiled at the thought of how astute I had become at judging potential buyers' taste in music, and how deftly I found the station they were most certain to hate by twiddling the knobs on the old and much loved tan leather Roberts radio set that had once been my father's. "I'm pretty sure that this couple won't be back, what with the music blaring and the tomato cans. But it was the bee that really finished things off for the wife. After that, her husband didn't stand a chance." I reached for the bottle and poured another glass for Angela and myself. "Still, it can't last forever. Someone will go for it sooner or later."

"So long as it's Italians who come to look, and especially Italians from the towns around here, I think you might be all right," said Angela. "Most Italians these days want something modern and clean. The women especially can't stand dust and they think these old places are a sign of poverty."

The sun was beginning to set over the blue-hazed hills in the distance, spreading a warm red glow along the horizon as the last of the cicadas fell silent.

"September already. The evenings are beginning to draw in, and the hunting season will be starting again in a few days." Angela picked up the now empty bottle and glasses and starting to move inside. "I must be going back to the village to see how Ercolino is doing making his pesto from all the basil he's grown this summer. Why don't you come up and have supper with us? We have to go back to look after Mamma in Terni tomorrow."

The thought of dinner with this hospitable couple was very tempting indeed. I knew there would be food that I could only dream of producing in my still very basic kitchen, as well as lively conversation as Ercolino worked himself up on some subject or another and Angela sought to introduce a note of common sense. But the following day I was due in Rome to work a shift in the newsroom of the English language newspaper, the *International Courier.* I had a very early start ahead of me and I needed to get a good night's sleep.

The connection had been through George, who was good friends with the editor, a fellow American, and I had been working there three days a week for the past fortnight. It brought in a welcome regular, if small income and also gave me a chance to meet people outside the particular world of San Massano.

I had decided to go by car early next morning, as it was a beautiful drive through the small towns and villages along the old Flaminian Way. And once in the *centro storico* of Rome itself, I got a curious thrill out of bombing through the narrow streets in my Fiat 500, rattling past the police checks put up to stop people like me without a permit from entering. I especially enjoyed it when I managed to get one of the policemen to climb down from his little box and run after me, in vain, of course, as I slammed down the accelerator and raced gaily off into the distance.

The day at the newspaper was hard work but fun, mainly because of the small but friendly group of young people who worked in the newsroom, which was housed in a fine old *palazzo* on Via della Ripetta, one of central Rome's most gracious avenues. The arts reporter, Andrew, a Scot who had lived in Rome for six years, made a point of showing me his favourite lunchtime venue, a tiny grocery store with three tables in an alleyway a five minute walk from the newspaper. It was run by a white-haired woman with strong hands, who briskly carved off a hunk of roast pork and crackling and stuffed it into two huge rolls while the husband filled a carafe with amber coloured wine from a cask behind the counter.

At last, bread with salt in it. The combination of the crusty bread and the fennel-roasted *porchetta* was sublime.

"They'll make up any sandwich you like here and they're all quite exceptional," said Andrew, who told me had been a lawyer in Edinburgh before he fell in love with Rome during a holiday there with his wife. She hadn't shared his enthusiasm for the move and the couple were now divorced. Andrew had thick dishevelled black hair and craggy features, inherited, he said, from his mother who was of Spanish descent and lived in a genteel Georgian flat in Cheltenham.

"We must come back and try their roast beef sandwich the next time you are in town. When do you work your next shift?"

For the time being at least, I was keen to keep my shifts at the paper to a maximum of three days a week, partly because however much I was learning to love the strangely beguiling chaos of Rome, I longed to be back in San Massano and to see work advancing on the house. I had also begun to make some good contacts with newspapers in England, America, Canada and Australia and some of them were starting to take regular pieces, so I needed to keep some spare time in hand. My latest commission was for a magazine in London. The editor wanted a feature I had suggested on a colourful Italian businessman called Silvio Berlusconi, who had once been a singer on a cruise ship and now controlled most of the media in Italy. Developments in the case of the Turkish assassin who had shot the pope in St. Peter's Square were always a good seller, and the trial brought almost daily revelations. Had he been working alone or was he part of a conspiracy mounted by the Soviet Union to punish the Polish pontiff for his allegiance to the Solidarity movement? The story virtually wrote itself.

I had now got the task of sending my articles from the back of Tito's shop down to a fine art. The shopkeeper always eyed me suspiciously as I came through the door with my computer under my arm, but I worked out that if I talked loudly all the time I was in the phone cabin, it made him less anxious. Even so, he still couldn't quite understand how I could have such long phone conversations without ever running up a bill.

"It beats me how you can talk to America without paying anything," he would say as I emerged from the cabin and he scanned the metre, which remained stubbornly set at zero. Of course, this method of filing stories only worked when Tito's shop was open, and if no one else was in a hurry to use the village's single telephone. Luckily, Tito worked long hours and, unless he was engaged in one of his twice-weekly calls to Clara, the phone booth was generally free. If only the news editors in the busy newsrooms around the world knew where their stories were coming from!

"So what's he like then?" Ercolino was having to shout above the noise in the packed room.

"What's who like?" I shouted back. An ample lady elbowed me from behind and called out to her husband who was much further back in the long queue.

"Giorgio, get a move on and come up next to me or we'll be here all night." The husband obediently shoved past me and pushed in front of a small man further ahead, who had been distracted as he studied the fistful of bills that he clutched in his hands.

"This journalist fellow. What's his name? Andrew isn't it?"

The way Ercolino rolled his tongue when he said the name left no doubt about what he thought, even though he had yet to meet him.

"Oh him. He's all right."

"Well you've mentioned his name at least three times already this morning."

"Have I? Ercolino, exactly how much more time are we going to have to stand in this queue?"

It had been Ercolino's idea to take me to the bank in Terni that morning to show me what people had to go through to pay their gas, water and electricity bills. Up until now, he had been paying my bills for me, but like a father talking to a lazy teenager, he said it was time I saw for myself just what was involved. The scene, when we reached the bank at nine in the morning, was like the first day of the January sales in London. Men and women were jostling for the best position, pushing each other so as to move closer to the counter, where a row of eight or so bank tellers were looking increasingly flustered.

"And all this, just to pay a few bills? Why don't they use direct debit? That's how I pay the bills for my house back in England."

"Direct debit? You must be joking! You won't see that for a long time. People take a day off work to pay their bills here, and that's once every two months. That's the way things work here so you'd better get used to it. Look out, that fat lady is trying to push in front of you. You've got a lot to learn about the art of queuing in Italy my darlin!"

Ercolino could never quite manage the *g* in ing. He grinned so that his eyes all but disappeared into the strong laugh lines etched deeply into the upper half of his face.

"Come on, once we've got this over we'll go for a nice coffee in the bar on Corso Tacito and you can tell me all about this fellow Andrew."

It turned out that I had a lot to learn about ordering a cup of coffee too. I had insisted on buying Ercolino his standard *caffe' corretto* – espresso laced with Sambuca liqueur – and he watched with amusement as I attempted to attract the busy waiter's attention. The bar, a few doors down, was almost as crowded as the bank as people rewarded themselves with coffee and pastries for the ordeal they had just endured.

"*Scusi*. Excuse me. Could I please have…?"

The waiter looked at me for a split second before his gaze passed to someone behind me with a louder voice and started clattering small cups and saucers on the counter.

"Actually it was my turn. *Per favore, un cappuccino e un caffe' corretto.*"

Again the waiter ignored me to serve someone on my left. How could anything so simple be so complicated? I knew the words I was using were right, so why didn't he listen to me?

"Oh come on now!" That was one of Ercolino's favourite expressions. "This is how you do it." And though Ercolino was a full head shorter than I was, he raised his hand, called to the waiter and ordered the coffees in a tone that made it clear he meant to be obeyed.

"*Subito*," said the waiter. He scuttled off to get the saucers, and placed my *cappuccino* and Ercolino's *caffe' corretto* on them with a small bow of his head.

"You see, in Italy you can get anything you want, but you have to be firm – and smile at the same time. You'll soon get the hang of it. Now drink your *cappuccino* before it gets cold. On the way home, I want to show you a very special place that I think you'll like."

"You'll never be able to go to the lake again if you decide to leave now." Ercolino's voice had a vein of childish spite in it that I had never heard before.

"No more afternoons spent in your boat. No more swims. It's too bloody cold to have a boat in England, that's for sure."

"La Scocciante". I murmured weakly. It had been Ercolino who had decided on the name of the boat that day he had taken me to Lake Piediluco.

***

The view of Piediluco as Ercolino's *Cinquecento* rounded the curve was like something out of one of the paintings we had studied at school when we were doing the Renaissance in history. The long ribbon of a lake was flanked on one side by a tiny village, while at the far end, another collection of honey-coloured houses and a church clung to the side of the hill, giving the strange impression that the painter had not quite got to grips with the perspective. Behind the soft-domed hill rose a towering mountain, with the first snow dusting its peak.

"Quite a sight, isn't it?" said Ercolino. He shifted the walnut gearstick into neutral and turned off the engine.

"What are you doing?" I looked at him nervously as the little car picked up speed and flew round a long series of curves and past a ruined castle.

"Don't worry." Ercolino did one of his eye-disappearing grins. "It's another Italian trick. "Saves petrol, saves money. I always do it when I'm going downhill."

It took less than half an hour for me to make what Ercolino immediately told me was a "bloody stupid" decision.

"What do you want to buy a bloody boat for? You drive me up the bend."

"Just a little rowing boat. It would be such fun taking it out on the lake and rowing across to one of these *trattorias*." I pointed to a small cluster of pretty lakeside restaurants, with tables and chairs set outside to catch the last of the late autumn sun.

"You won't catch me going out in one of those things. I can't even swim."

One of the biggest wrenches in leaving Brighton had been having to sell the small sailing dinghy that Rob and I had bought together and affectionately christened Eric. It had a red wooden hull and pale blue sails and would race along with the waves thudding against its bows on the way to Brighton beach from Shoreham where we kept it.

"No, I really would like a boat. Let's go and see if that rental place has anything to sell."

Grumbling under his breath, Ercolino followed as I made my way down some steep narrow steps where six or seven bright blue wooden motorboats were tied up. Half-way down, a good-looking Italian boy in his early twenties was busily engaged in kissing his girlfriend, whose long dark brown curls were all that could be seen.

"I thought this was a Catholic country? I didn't know young Italians behaved like that." I was surprised to see such a public embrace.

"You'd be amazed what we Italians get up to," said Ercolino. "This is the country of love, not like England, where you're all so bloody cold. Hey *ragazzo*. Put the girl down for a minute and come and talk to us. My friend here wants to buy a boat."

I found myself singing as I drove along the country lanes back to San Massano much later that day. The acquisition of the little boat had lifted my spirits.

"We'll call her *La Scocciante*," Ercolino had said after he had helped negotiate a surprisingly good price with the boat hire boy. It was a small fibreglass skiff, and after a few minutes' discussion, the boy agreed to throw in free mooring as well. He was clearly anxious to get back to his girlfriend.

"What does *Scocciante* mean?

"It means someone who's a pain in the harse, just like you." He turned to look at me and ruffled my hair. "You know I don't mean it. Come on now, Angela's at home and she'll be waiting for us for lunch."

Angela had placed a steaming dish of pasta with Ercolino's home-made walnut pesto on the table.

"You look very happy. What have you been up to?"

I explained about the boat.

"All I need now is a horse and life will be just about perfect," I said.

"Why do you want a horse? You don't need a bloody horse. You need a boyfriend!" Ercolino leapt up from his seat at the end of the table and started pouring red wine from a plain glass bottle.

"Oh Ercolino" Mamma's voice was still strong, in between long sips from her tumbler of wine. "Why are you getting so worked up?"

"The point is *Mamma*," said Ercolino switching to Italian. "That this girl is messing about with boats and horses, when it's time she settled down."

The drive home from Terni took me past a series of lay-bys, each one marked by a camper van. It had taken some time to work out why they were there and for a long while I had puzzled over the fact that the drivers were always women. The truth suddenly dawned on me one day when a middle-aged man with a paunch emerged from the side door, looked both ways furtively and quickly climbed into a white Fiat Punto that had been parked alongside. Soon afterwards, the camper van's owner settled back into the driver's seat and reached for a book of crosswords and a pen from behind the sun visor. With a plump face and thickset frame, squeezed into a bottle green woollen jumper that was several sizes too small, she looked at least sixty, maybe more. She propped a pair of gilt framed spectacles on her nose and settled down to while away the time until her next customer arrived.

Angela had a point. Everyone really was at it around here, it seemed.

My heart sank when I saw Primo's silver Mercedes parked outside his house as I turned the last corner on the small winding round that ended in San Massano. That was sure to mean more discussions about resurfacing the drive and I really didn't have the stomach for it just now. I had to be up early next day for another shift on the Rome newspaper and the last thing I needed was to be called over to the pink house. Be firm with a smile, I said to myself, remembering Ercolino's mantra. I got out of my car and guiltily put my head down and strode swiftly up the slope towards my house.

"CLAY!"

Be firm with a smile.

I smiled, and turned round to face Nadia, who was walking towards me with uncertain steps in a pair of fuchsia suede boots, pulled up over cream coloured leggings. She stretched out a bangled hand to reveal nails varnished to match her boots.

"*Ciao bella.* I just wanted to ask you…"

"Oh hello Nadia. I'm afraid I'm in rather a hurry, so I can't stop right now." Be firm, but with a smile. I smiled at Nadia, noticing that her lipstick exactly matched both her boots and the nail varnish.

Her own smile faded slightly.

"Oh, what a shame. I just wanted to tell you that the hunting season starts tomorrow. So you'll hear rather a lot of noise. Primo's organising a shoot for wild boar and he's terribly excited about it. To be honest, I find it all rather tedious and I was hoping you'd come and keep me company. We could spend the morning looking through some of the fashion magazines I've brought with me."

I told Nadia that I would be leaving for Rome early in the morning and her face fell.

"Oh well, it means another day on my own in this dreadful place," she said despondently. "There isn't even a phone so I can talk to my friends. Anyway, why don't you come round when you get back? Primo's hunting friends will all be staying for dinner, worst luck, so I could do with some moral support."

The next morning, a volley of loud shots woke me long before the time I had set my alarm. I stretched out a hand and blearily looked at the luminescent hands of the small plastic clock perched on the chair at the side of my bed. Organising a bedside table was still fairly low on my long list of priorities. Four-thirty. What was going on?

Another barrage of shots burst out from somewhere uncomfortably close by. It sounded as if someone was firing from right below my bedroom window. Pulling a thick cardigan around my shoulders I gingerly opened the shutters and looked out into the early morning mist. Dawn was just breaking, though there was no sound of birdsong, and in the half-light I could just make out several figures in the garden below. They seemed to be dressed in army fatigues and each man had a long rifle in one hand and several rounds of ammunition looped over his shoulder. One of them held a large walkie-talkie in his other hand and put it to his mouth. The signal made a piercing sound.

"Primo. Are you reading me? There has been a sighting of three, repeat three members of the enemy. We are on their trail. Over."

"Good work Luigi. Don't let them escape. Over."

"We are engaging with them now. Over."

"Let me know if you need support from other ranks. We are covering your rear flank. Over and out."

Wretched hunters. Why did they have to get up at such a ridiculous hour? But as my irritability wore off, it occurred to me that they had probably done me a favour waking me up so early. It meant I would now have time for a *cappuccino* and *cornetto* at my favourite bar near the newspaper office before I went into work, instead of rushing up the flight of stairs at the last minute, and working all morning on an empty stomach. The thought of the heady aroma of fresh coffee being ground and the sugary taste of the soft white croissant that the bar brought in each morning from a nearby bakery galvanised me into action. Within a few minutes I was dressed and ready, and cautiously descending the steep stone steps I peered round the corner of the arch that opened up into my front garden. The tops of several green and white camouflage hats could just be made out from behind a few bushes. On the outer edges, where my garden butted onto a small wood, red and white plastic tape had been strung between trees, making it look as if it was a crime scene. At intervals along the cordon, an orange and white cardboard notice proclaimed: *Danger! Wild board hunt in progress. Signed: The Invincibles!*

The rest of the autumn passed in a blaze of bright yellow, orange and vermillion. The days were still warm most of the time, but once the sun went down, a relentless chill set in, working its way through the thick stone walls of my house and into my bed and the clothes I left at the end of it when I went to sleep at night. I would have given anything for the electric blanket I had on my bed back in Brighton in winter, but though I had searched all the electrical shops here, I had yet to find one. I fell into a pattern of going to Rome to work my three weekly shifts and spending the rest of the time in San Massano, where the contrast could not have been greater. In Rome, there were so many people on the busy, noisy streets it was sometimes easier to dodge past the cars parked on the pavement and walk in the road to get somewhere quickly. In San Massano, with winter rapidly closing in, most people spent their time sitting around the log fire, chatting, cooking dinner and playing cards, and I could sometimes go several days without seeing a soul.

Aside from the Rome newspaper, my new career as a freelance foreign correspondent was taking off. I had found out that the Palestinian terrorists who had recently hijacked a cruise liner off Egypt and been captured and flown to Italy were now being held in the top security prison inside the Castle of Spoleto. Natalino's aunt worked as a cleaner in the prison, and with intercession from her nephew, I got a good story about the terrorists' arrival by armoured truck, what they looked like, how they spent their days and exercised in the massive courtyard, and even what they had for lunch and dinner. The only victim of the attack had been an elderly paralysed man from New York, who had been thrown over the side of the ship in his wheelchair, so several American newspapers were keen to have my story.

After long hours spent huddled over my tiny computer at the formica kitchen table, I would often go for long walks to warm myself up. These invariably turned into an adventure, as I had little idea of where I was going and still found it hard to get my bearings once I had wandered off the paths that I knew. In almost all the villages, snarling dogs prowled through the narrow alleyways, barking menacingly at anyone who dared to set foot on their territory. There was talk amongst the farmers that wolves were starting to be glimpsed in the mountains again after an absence of several years.

One late November afternoon, I became hopelessly lost in the woods on the hill across the valley from my house. I had often looked at it from my kitchen window, and wondered what it would be like to tramp along the tracks covered with the russet coloured leaves that had formed such a spectacle that magnificent autumn. But as darkness crowded in, and the vegetation became more and more impenetrable, I realised I was in danger of staying there all night. Whichever way I turned I came up against a thick mesh of climbers, overgrown shrubs and brambles the size of a man's finger, which tore into my hands and wrists. I had no idea in which direction I should be pointing and was beginning to feel very cold. If only I had left my kitchen light on. At least it would have given me some idea of which way to aim for. In the end, it was another light that saved me. A few hundred yards from where I was standing, a pair of yellow headlights beamed out into the darkness and the sound of a diesel engine being started broke the silence. Hunters again, but this time I was very glad to see them. I called out loudly and they came over with torches, using sticks to break through a path to where I was now well and truly trapped.

"*Signorina*. Whatever are you doing out here at this time of night? Haven't you got a home to go to?" One of the two hunters passed me a flask containing a fiery bitter liquid. He led the way back to a tiny four-wheel drive Panda, a car used by many farmers and woodsmen around here to drive along the narrowest, muddiest tracks. "Here, drink some of my home-made grappa. You must be the English *signorina*. My cousin

Agostino told me about you. Come on, let's get you back. You look half frozen to death."

In Rome, Andrew was my constant companion, showing me some of the many corners that he had discovered over the years which, he said, made the city so captivating. I was beginning to agree. At first, the unruly din at every turn had been overwhelming and I had not taken to the city. On the streets, it was impossible to have a conversation due to the constant flow of buses and cars and impatient horn-blowing as drivers found themselves in gridlock, which appeared to happen very often. As a result, people took to shouting as the natural mode of communication. The most ordinary exchange between two people was invariably conducted at a volume several decibels higher than normal, and for some reason, Romans always seemed to be cross when they spoke to each other. But as I began to explore some of the hidden piazzas and narrow streets, often with some enchanting bars and *trattorias*, the city started to cast a powerful spell over me. We had now exhausted the rich array of sandwiches offered by the grocery store near the newspaper office, and, at Andrew's enthusiastic suggestion, had moved on to a small *vino e cucina* run by another elderly couple who lived out in the Castelli Romani, the pretty cluster of volcanic hill villages just south of Rome, where the pope had his summer residence.

"I've been coming here for years and this couple are very special," said Andrew one lunchtime in December. The lady he affectionately called Granny had brought us a paper tablecloth and a flask of straw-coloured white wine from nearby Frascati. "They drive in every morning, rain or shine, in their little *Ape*, with all the food for the day in the back. You have to have whatever Granny has prepared, but it's always delicious."

Today's menu was a dish of white butter beans, simmered in a rich tomato sauce flavoured with thick strips of bacon fat, followed by a plate of squid with peas cooked in a white wine sauce. When she cleared our plates, Granny brought us a big tin box to the table and fished out two round biscuits each, the middle hollowed out and the tops sprinkled with sugar.

"They're to dunk in the rest of your wine," said Andrew. We got out our money to pay the ridiculously small bill. "Oh well, time to get back to the grindstone, I suppose."

Back in the office, there were scenes of confusion. As we came through the door, the news editor was walking hurriedly out of the editor's office.

"Quick, get to your desk and start writing. We need a thousand words for tomorrow's front page," he thrust a sheaf of papers torn from the newswire into my hand. "Andrew, you're going to have to help too. Check the wires constantly. This is a case of all hands on deck. There's been a terrorist attack at Fiumicino airport."

It was a hectic afternoon and a sad one too. Among the victims killed when terrorists opened fire on passengers in the lounge of Rome's main airport was the young daughter of the news editor of the Associated Press in Rome. The foreign press corps in the city was very tight-knit and everyone knew each other. By eight o'clock that evening, the special edition was ready to go to press for distribution early the next morning. Nothing remained but to have a quick beer in the bar downstairs with Andrew and head for home.

"It's late. You shouldn't drive at this time of night, especially in that old car," said Andrew. We sat at a small marble table drinking bottles of *Peroni*.

"My car's fine. It never lets me down," I defended my Fiat 500 stoutly.

"You could always stay at my place. It's much closer than driving all the way back to your village." He closed his large hand over mine where it rested on the table.

I removed it gently and picked up the bottle to finish my beer before getting up to go.

"No thanks Andrew. I'll see you next week."

Damn, damn, damn! Why hadn't I kept my mouth shut? I banged the steering wheel in frustration, before turning the ignition and pressing the starter button one last time, though I knew it was useless. Now what was I going to do? I was in the middle of nowhere, still a good 20 kilometres from San Massano and it was nearly ten o'clock. I fumbled in my bag and reluctantly pulled out the business card for Dirty Paolo. I didn't really have much choice. There was a roadside bar a few hundred yards further along from where my car had stopped on a lonely country road. It had a telephone sign outside. The metal shutters were being drawn down noisily from within, but if I moved quickly I might just make it. I suppose I should be grateful that Dirty Paolo lived over the shop. But why him, of all people?

Less than three quarters of an hour later, Dirty Paolo was shining his torch under the bonnet and pulling various leads to find out what was wrong. I tried not to notice that he had changed out of his normal mechanics' overalls and was wearing a pair of carefully pressed jeans and a dark blue mohair sweater.

"There's the problem, *Signorina*. It's your fan belt," he said triumphantly. He took off his glasses and turned towards me, flashing me a smile.

"So when can you fix it?"

"Not tonight, that's for sure. I don't have the piece with me." Was I mistaken, or did he seem pleased as he said this? "But I can give you a lift back home in my car. Then we can come back together in the morning and fetch yours."

The journey home seemed to take forever, punctuated, all too predictably, by Dirty Paolo's errant hand, which wandered over on to my knee every so often. Each time, I placed his hand firmly back on his side of the car and asked him to leave me alone. Be firm, with a smile, though it was hard to smile in these conditions.

"I'm sorry. But you're so very pretty. I just can't help myself," he said, tapping the steering wheel irritatingly in time to a mawkish tune he had fed into the tape deck. "This is where you live isn't it? What a cold lonely place it looks!" He drew up at the bottom of my drive. "Just one little kiss? No? Oh well. I'll pick you up at nine o'clock in the morning and maybe you'll have changed your mind."

The return journey next morning to fetch my car was a carbon copy of the one the previous evening. I couldn't have made it clearer how tiresome I found his advances, but Dirty Paolo kept on trying regardless, smiling as though it was quite normal behaviour. To his credit, he replaced the faulty fan belt quickly and efficiently, and after asking, for the umpteenth time, if I'd like to go to lunch with him at a nice little restaurant he knew just round the corner, he accepted my refusal with a magnanimous grin and a shrug of the shoulders and presented me with a bill that would hardly have covered his petrol there and back.

"Forgive me. But you can't blame me for trying *Signorina*. I'm only human," he said and climbed back into his car. "Your car should be fine now, but you know you can always count on Paolo if anything goes wrong with it. Paolo's always here to help, especially a *bella signorina* in distress."

I decided not to tell Angela and Ercolino about Dirty Paolo when I dropped in at their Terni apartment on the way home to San Massano. I hadn't forgotten what had happened when Ercolino has got to hear about the advances of the restaurant owner from Fiore, when I had been painting the kitchen that day not long after my arrival. I had carelessly recounted the episode one evening, when Cesare and Mirella were having dinner with us all. Ercolino and Cesare had gone into a huddle together, before mysteriously disappearing for a good half hour. When they came back they both appeared hot and flustered, but with a look of satisfaction on their faces.

"He won't be doing that again in a hurry, molesting women who have chosen to live here in my country," said Cesare, his scout's scarf slightly skewed now on his massive chest.

"No, he certainly won't," added Ercolino, who was half Cesare's size and appeared to have a graze on one of his knuckles. "Don't worry, we've given that bloody man a big black eye. And when his wife finds out, she'll probably give him another one."

Ercolino was in no mood to do me any favours that day. Soon after I walked through their front door, which was always left unlocked with the key on the outside, Angela greeted me with an affectionate hug and sat me down at the kitchen table where lunch was just about to be served. But Ercolino's usually smiling face looked like thunder and he turned on me furiously, waving a wad of papers under my nose.

"What the bloody hell have you been doing, driving around Rome and getting all these fines?" His face was turning from pink to purple and he was working himself up into a temper. "Don't you know that the car's in my name, so the fines all come to me? There's 300,000 lire worth of fines here for driving through the centre without a permit."

"But I thought they hadn't caught me."

"The trouble is, you didn't think at all. You English are all the same. You think you can come to Italy and do what you like. But we're not all so bloody stupid you know."

Ercolino had a point. There was something about being in Italy that turned everyday life into one big game. That was part

112

of the attraction of course. I often used to jump on a bus without a ticket. It was partly because I couldn't be bothered to go to the *edicola* – the newsstands where they sell them. But in my heart of hearts, I know it was really the thrill of trying to get away with something that would have been unthinkable back in England.

After much cajoling from Angela and Mamma, and a plate of his favourite *ciriole* with mushrooms, Ercolino came round in the end and promised to talk to a friend who was a policeman, and try to get the fines stopped. The lunchtime news, which we watched as we drank a short dark espresso, was all about the aftermath of the Fiumicino attack, with graphic footage of the destruction and photographs of the victims. While still at the Rome newspaper office, I had taken advantage of its more sophisticated telephone system to send over a piece to my regular newspaper clients and I had got commissions to write a big feature on the drama from several Sunday newspapers. It was time to get to work.

It was bitterly cold in my house now and I had transferred my writing sessions from the kitchen, where there was no heat at all, to a small table in the sitting room, next to the log fire which was the only source of warmth. Wearing a pair of Fagin gloves with the finger ends cut off, two sweaters and a brown woollen Marks and Spencer cardigan that had belonged to my father, I sat hunched over my computer, writing about the attack, the victims, preparations for the funerals and investigations into the Palestinian terrorists believed to be behind the killings. I was so engrossed in the story that it took some time to register that someone was knocking on the door. The knocking had turned to banging and reluctantly I stood up. Two *carabinieri* were standing outside, looking important in their smart black and red uniforms. I recognised them as the same pair who had bundled Generosa into the police car that day in the piazza.

"*Buonasera Signorina*. We have an urgent communication for

you." The taller policeman handed me a green card, with my name on it and an address in Terni. "You are ordered to report to the police station in Terni first thing tomorrow at this address."

"But I can't. I'm writing an important article and tomorrow's the deadline."

"That is of no interest to us," said the other *carabiniere* in a stiff tone. "We have been instructed to pass these orders on to you, and should you decide to disobey, I cannot answer for the consequences."

"I really can't come tomorrow morning," I said firmly, remembering at the last minute to smile as well. This time, Ercolino's advice wasn't working.

"*Signorina*, perhaps you haven't understood. You have no choice."

"All foreign residents everywhere in Italy are being called in to their nearest police stations," said the slightly less aggressive officer. "It's to do with check-ups following the Fiumicino terror attack."

"But what have I got to do with the Fiumicino attack? I'm English, not Palestinian."

"Just make sure you are there tomorrow morning at 8.30 sharp," said the gruffer of the two. "Goodnight *Signorina*."

Several hours later, a glass of whisky on one side of my writing table to keep me warm and a mug of black coffee on the other side to keep me from falling asleep, I put the final touches to my long feature about the airport killings. Although I was sorely tempted not to go to the police station tomorrow, something told me that the repercussions would be very serious indeed.

Suddenly, there was the sound of another knock at the door. This was beginning to smack of police harassment. I got up sharply and opened the door abruptly. No smile this time.

"There's no need to keep pestering me," I said furiously.

"Oh sorry. I certainly didn't mean to pester you. It's just that I was staying with my cousin in Spoleto and thought I'd look you up."

In the half-light of the doorstep, it was hard to make out who the visitor was. It certainly wasn't the *carabinieri*.

"Don't you remember me? It's Mario. We met at George's party in the summer. But I can see that it's not a good time. I'm very sorry for disturbing you."

Chapter Six

The next morning, I was Tito's first customer. Dressed smartly as always in his white coat he pulled up the shutters and looked surprised to see me standing on the steps.

"What brings you here so early, *Signorina*? Is everything all right?

"Yes thanks Tito. Well actually not really. I've got to go down to Terni to the police station, and first I need to make an urgent phone call."

"The police station! You're not in any trouble are you?" He eyed the computer tucked under my arm. "Oh, it's one of those phone calls. Come on then, you know where to go. But please *Signorina*, don't run my bill up will you? I'm going to need all the money I have to pay for the wedding. Clara's talking of inviting the whole village. And that includes you of course. Now don't think I'm prying, but what's all this about the police? They're to be avoided at all costs if you ask me. Come to think of it, Clara's uncle Giovanni works at the *Questura* in Terni. He's something quite important. He might be able to help if you get stuck."

Tito followed me as I made my way to the back of the shop. I stepped into the tiny booth and pulled my computer out of its case. He was watching me intently.

"I think I just heard someone come into the shop Tito." What a stroke of luck. A shrill voice was calling his name.

"Tito. Where are you? Get a move on. I've run out of coffee and Luigi needs his *caffelatte*."

The connection was better than usual this morning, and by the time I heard Tito's brisk footsteps returning in my direction the window on the tiny computer screen told me that the transmission was nearly finished. Ten seconds, nine, eight, seven.

"How's it going *Signorina*? Do you need any help? Can't you get through? I see the metre is still on zero."

Transmission completed. I wrenched the phone receiver out of the coupler and shoved the computer back into its case.

"No, everything's fine thanks Tito. I must run, or I'll be late for the police, and they told me to be there by 8.30 on the dot."

"Don't forget to ask for Giovanni if you have any problems. His surname is Bruschi. Colonel Giovanni Bruschi. Tell him I gave you his name."

My little Fiat 500 spun round the corners as we coasted down the country lanes. I had taken to using Ercolino's trick of switching off the engine on the downhill stretches, putting her into second gear and starting the motor as we rounded the bend before driving into Lavena.

Entire family dies after eating poisoned mushrooms.

The billboard outside the newsagent caught my eye as we sped past. No time to buy a newspaper right now. I had just ten minutes to get to Terni, and I had a feeling that it wouldn't be wise to turn up late.

The encounter at the police station proved even worse than I had expected.

"Well *Signorina*, as I'm sure you can understand, we need to check the movements of all foreigners on our territory at the moment, in the light of recent tragic events. But I can't find any record of you having registered with us." The *carabiniere* was thumbing through a massive pile of manila files on his desk. I had been ordered to sit on an uncomfortable metal chair facing him.

117

"Why should I have registered?"

The policeman paused from his search in the files and glared at me coldly. His eyes narrowing, he reached for a cigarette from a leather case and lit it carefully.

"Surely, *Signorina*, you must know that, as in any country, you have to register your presence here."

He must have seen my look of bewilderment.

"I assume you are familiar with article 242 of the law on terrorism?"

"I'm afraid I don't know what you are talking about."

He flicked the ash of his cigarette into a ceramic ashtray with a gaudy painting of the waterfalls on its base. It was clear he was beginning to lose his patience.

"*Signorina*, show me your documents please."

I drew my passport out of my bag and placed it on the desk.

"And your *permesso di soggiorno*."

"What is a *permesso di soggiorno*?"

"A *permesso di soggiorno* is the foreigner's permit that you have to carry on your person at all times, by law, and show whenever you are asked to by a public official."

"But I don't have one. No one ever told me I would need one."

The *carabiniere* sucked in his breath in disbelief and stubbed out his cigarette. He picked up the receiver of a solid grey telephone on the corner of his desk.

"Sonia. Put me through to the *comandante's* office at once. We have a case here of a foreigner with no *permesso di soggiorno*."

"You do realise, *Signorina*, that you are in very grave trouble?" He looked at me with a menacing stare, the receiver still in one hand as he waited to be put through. "As a foreigner, you have a legal duty to register with the police within 24 hours of entering the country. It's standard procedure. How else are we supposed to keep track of terrorists?"

I was about to ask if terrorists also registered when they

entered Italian territory, but the expression on the police officer's face made me think twice.

"This is an extremely serious offence, you understand. It carries with it a fine of one million lire and immediate deportation."

"But I have a house here. I'm in the middle of doing it up. You can't just send me away."

"That is exactly what we can do, *Signorina*. The law is very clear. You should have thought of the consequences before you decided to break it."

A man's voice could be heard on the other end of the telephone. The *carabiniere's* brow furrowed as he listened, occasionally interjecting with: "*Si comandante*". At last, he finished with a respectful "*Subito comandante*" and replaced the receiver before turning back to me.

"You have been very fortunate, *Signorina*." He twirled a ballpoint pen in his hand and reached for a sheet of paper. "It seems you have well-placed connections. If you would kindly present the following items in the next forty eight hours, I will personally attend to the issue of a *permesso di soggiorno* for you. He scribbled a few lines: passport, 3 photocopies; 4 photographs, signed on the back, application form for *permesso di soggiorno*, 3 photocopies. He smiled courteously and stood up, his peaked cap under one arm.

"And now, please allow me to escort you to the door. My secretary will provide you with the forms and you can arrange with her when to return them. Please don't hesitate to contact me if you encounter any difficulties. *Buongiorno Signorina*."

A note was pinned on the door of my house when I got home much later that day.

Missed you again. Better luck next time. Ciao Mario.

With all the drama of my summons to the police station, I had completely forgotten about his visit the night before. Mario must think me very unfriendly. I wondered what he was doing here. George was away, and wasn't due back for several weeks.

I didn't have to wait long to find out. Less than half an hour later the sound of a car hurtling up the rocky drive jolted me out of my thoughts. I had been reflecting, for the umpteenth time since exiting the police station, on my lucky escape. How complicated life was in this country, where there seemed to be rules at every turn just waiting to trip you up. No wonder it was so important to have friends in the right places. And how fortunate that Clara's uncle had stepped in as my mystery benefactor. For it must have been him who had come to my rescue. I had a great deal to thank him for, and Tito too, who I could only imagine had called ahead and arranged it all after I had left that morning. I made a mental note to do more of my shopping from his store, even if it meant buying stale bread and cemetery candles that I didn't need.

My kitchen window, which had views over the hills and valleys in all directions, had the bonus of offering a perfect vantage point for inspecting visitors before they climbed the steep stone steps to my front door. On several occasions, the advance warning had proved useful, enabling me to pretend to be asleep, or out walking in the woods, when I hadn't felt like being disturbed. But there would be no need for any such ruse today. It would be a welcome relief to see a friendly face after the ordeal with the *carabinieri*, and from what little I knew of Mario, he appeared to be good company. His girlfriend was a less appealing prospect, and I could make out a second figure getting out of the passenger seat. Soon, the sound of two pairs of feet could be heard coming up the stairs. I was feeling in a magnanimous mood and I smiled as I opened the door to greet the couple.

"Ah, I've found you in at last," said Mario, a broad smile breaking out to reveal the perfectly-shaped teeth that I had noticed before. There was no girlfriend, but another, taller man was coming up the stairs behind him. He appeared to be finding the exertion something of a strain.

"I hope you don't mind. I've brought my cousin. We've been spending a few days in Spoleto."

The cousin stretched out a hand to shake mine, squeezing it with a firm grip and holding my elbow with his other hand.

"Aurelio. Very pleased to meet you. Those stairs are killers. No wonder you look in such good shape. Mario has told me all about the English damsel in the castle." Aurelio moved into the sitting room, then on into the kitchen to look out over the views. "But I never expected anything quite so spectacular. It's rather like being up in an eagle's nest."

"Actually it's the first time I've seen it too," said Mario. He followed his cousin to the kitchen window and gazed out. "Before, I was never allowed off the leash for long enough when I came to visit George."

"Oh, so how is, er, your girlfriend. Isn't she with you this time?" I knew we had been introduced briefly at the party, but I struggled to remember her name.

"Oh you mean the lovely Laura," Aurelio butted in, clearly amused at his cousin's discomfort. "That's one of the reasons we came here. To give Mario a chance to get away from her."

"That's not quite true. We just agreed to go our separate ways." Mario was looking even more uncomfortable now.

"You mean you decided," quipped Aurelio. "She had something quite different in mind." He started humming the wedding march. "Anyway, you could never have married her. She was far too boring. That would have been a life sentence."

It seemed like the right time to change the subject. The dying sun had sunk behind the soft hills in the distance and the crimson glow had turned to purple. I asked my guests if they wanted a drink and retrieved some wine glasses from the kitchen shelf. In spite of the precarious state of organisation in the house, I always made sure that I had decent glasses to drink out of, and these were heavy crystal goblets, a relic from my parents' home and among my most treasured possessions.

We toasted each other's health and sat down by the massive fireplace, where two big logs were burning fiercely. Aurelio was more heavily built than Mario, with a shock of dark brown curly hair. He started to tell me about his life in Bologna, where he had moved a few years earlier to take up a job with a bank. He lived with a girl called Arianna in a flat not far from the centre.

"Bologna has an appalling climate. It's either so hot that you can't think or it's so cold that it freezes all your bodily functions. But it does have its advantages, especially compared with Naples. Things work in Bologna, at least most of the time. And people can find jobs. You should come and spend a weekend with us. I know Arianna would be happy to meet you."

"Ah Arianna. You're a lucky man to have found her," said Mario. "God knows what someone as sweet as her sees in someone like you."

Aurelio made a dive for Mario, who deftly moved the crystal glass out of range before parrying the blow.

"We're only joking. You mustn't take us too seriously." Mario flashed one of his grins as he held Aurelio at arm's length.

"Mario is actually my favourite cousin, and I've got quite a lot of them," said Aurelio, giving his cousin a hug. "He's the sort of person who would do anything for someone he cares about. Now let's talk about serious matters. I'm starving. What are we going to do for dinner?"

An hour later, installed in the corner table of a small stone-built *trattoria* a ten-minute drive down the hill, we ate plates of what the bustling woman who ran the place said was home-made *pappardelle al cinghiale*, long pasta ribbons with a sauce made of wild boar.

"And afterwards *Signora*? What do you recommend for the next course?" It was Aurelio who asked the question.

"Aurelio's always hungry," said Mario. He poured me a glass of the dark red wine that had been placed on the table as soon as we sat down. There was no written menu, but the owner rattled off a list of dishes, most of which I had never heard of. Aurelio ordered a big platter of grilled meat for all of us to share, and asked for some roast potatoes to go with it.

"You wouldn't want to be a vegetarian around here would you?" said Mario smiling. He placed a massive pork chop on my plate.

Somehow, we managed to clear all the plates and the evening passed in an agreeable haze of food, more wine and good humoured banter. Aurelio talked far more than Mario, and he had a seemingly never ending source of anecdotes and merciless observations. Aurelio was exactly the same age as I was, while Mario was a couple of years younger. I felt very much at home in their company, although it was sometimes hard keeping up with the pace of the quips and the speed of the language. Aurelio was also a very good mimic, and even I could hear the difference in the accents as he passed from imitations of people from Bologna, Naples, Milan and the unmistakable country twang of the natives of this rural part of southern Umbria.

"Listen to this conversation that I overheard in the tobacconist's shop just down the road when I was buying some cigarettes before we came to see you," said Aurelio. We were now sipping grappa which the restaurant owner had brought to us on the house.

"These two men were talking, and you could see that one of them was a baker, because he still had one of those hats on that they always wear, and he was covered in flour. The other fellow must have been a farmer or something like that. So the farmer says to the baker:

'When do you find the time to sort out your wife, if you're always working?'

The baker put on a serious expression and said:

'I always give my wife a good poke on Saturday evenings, because I don't have to get up so early on a Sunday. That's the rule in our house.'

So the farmer replies:

'If you work out that there are fifty two weeks in the year, and sometimes she can't do it because of you-know-what, and sometimes she's got a headache, and sometimes you don't feel up to it, that probably makes about thirty times a year that you're giving her a poke. So if there are 365 days in the year, who is giving it to her the other 335 days?

The baker took off his hat and scratched his head.

'You've got a point there. I'd better give her a poke more often.'

"I was laughing so much I almost forgot what I'd gone into the shop for." Aurelio was laughing again at the thought of the strange conversation he had overheard. "The people round here are in another world. Long may it stay that way."

The *trattoria* was empty now and it was clearly time to go. Aurelio wouldn't hear of accepting anything to cover my share of the bill. Mario drove me home, Aurelio stretched out lazily in the back seat.

"*Arrivederci inglesina*. That was fun. Come and see us in Bologna," he said, leaning forward to give me a pat on the shoulder.

"Yes, that was a wonderful evening," said Mario. He was holding the door open for me and had parked in such a way that his headlights lit up the pitched black path, so that I could see where to go. "I haven't enjoyed myself so much for a very long time."

Neither, I reflected, had I.

It came as no real surprise when there was a knock on the door the following Friday and I opened it to see Mario. Not that I had been expecting him. We had left on very casual terms, with a peck on each cheek and a vague promise to keep in touch. Of course, there is no way he could have warned me that he was coming, since I had no telephone and he certainly didn't have Tito's number at the shop. A long time afterwards, Mario would ask me why I hadn't registered any kind of shock at seeing him standing there on my doorstep, unannounced.

"It was as if you knew I'd come back," he had said.

And maybe, buried far down somewhere deep inside me, I had known just that.

"Come in," I said, giving him another kiss on both cheeks as though it was the most natural thing in the world.

He was alone this time.

I had been very firm in my mind about what I did and didn't want at that time. I definitely wasn't interested in another relationship right now. And I certainly was not going to get involved in any way with an Italian man. Not that Mario was asking me to. He told me he was lonely, and that he enjoyed my company. Enough to get in his car and drive for more than three hours on the off chance that he would find me at home. But all that came out much later. First, there was the cocktail party conversation, stilted at first, and then more relaxed. What did I do? Where had I gone to school? University?

"It was always my dream to go to an English university, with a campus. Not like here, where you just live at home or in an apartment with other students."

By now, we had moved on, from the chairs by my fireplace to an elegant bar in the main piazza of Spoleto, where he had taken me for his favourite *aperitivo,* a Campari topped up with prosecco and soda water and served with lots of ice.

"So did you go? To university I mean?" I reached out to spear a large green olive from a small glass dish on the counter.

"Yes, and no. I started, but then it all became too difficult. You see my father died when I was sixteen and it was very

125

unexpected. He didn't have time to make any provision for me and my mother and sister. At first, we managed somehow, though we had to leave our apartment and move in with my mother's sister. But after a year at university it became very obvious that I would have to leave and get a job. It's one of my deepest regrets."

He passed me the dish of olives and I took another, listening as he spoke. He was far more talkative this evening than he has been the night we had gone out with Aurelio.

"So you went to Cambridge. Lucky you. I had a photograph of it on the front cover of my English text book at school. I'll never forget it, with all those daffodils and students riding around on bicycles. You wouldn't want to do that in Naples."

For dinner, we went back to the *trattoria* where we had been the week before with Aurelio. The woman who ran it remembered us and showed us to a small table by a blazing fire. Over plates of *orecchiette con cima di rape* – small pieces of pasta with broccoli laced with garlic and dried chilli, we chatted about our very different lives. It would be hard to find two people with such dissimilar backgrounds, but there were some things we did have in common, good and not so good. Fathers who had died when they were far too young, for one thing. Neither of us needed to go into too much detail about the pain of that, but I supposed Mario's situation had been worse than mine as he had lost his home and his place at university as well. At least he still had his mother. On the plus side, it soon emerged that Mario loved sport. He was a very keen water polo player and a member of the local team in Naples. That accounted for the strikingly broad shoulders which seemed out of place on his otherwise slight frame.

"How about tennis?" I hadn't had a game since I left England, though I'd always played a couple of times a week in Brighton and I missed it now.

"One of my favourite sports, though I haven't played for a

126

while. I'll bring my racquet up next time I come. Whoever loses pays for lunch. So you'd better get your money ready."

I laughed.

"Don't be so sure. But it's a deal." Suddenly, I realised we were already talking about the next time we would see each other.

It was far too late for Mario to drive back to Naples that night, and although breathalysers had yet to appear in this part of Italy, it made no sense at all for him to drive such a long distance after drinks in the bar and a bottle of wine at the restaurant.

"I've got a spare bedroom you can have," I said. We were driving back to San Massano, rather too fast for my liking. If I had one criticism of my new friend it was his driving. "It's pretty basic, but you're lucky, there's a bed, which is more than there was a few weeks ago."

"Luxury," he murmured half an hour later. I looked at him to see if he was serious and he smiled back. "No really. I've seen worse. I'll be fine. Is there any chance of a blanket?"

I fetched the only spare blanket I had, a rather flimsy one, I noticed guiltily.

"Well, I'd better turn in. It's late and the people from the phone company are coming tomorrow morning," I said. "There's a good chance they are going to extend the phone line down as far as my house. They told me to stay in all morning and wait for the visit."

"That sounds like something to celebrate," said Mario. "Goodnight. See you in the morning."

At the time, there was a part of me that was surprised when Mario didn't make a move that night. All the ingredients were there: the feel-good factor from the evening spent at the restaurant, the intimacy of being alone in a big old house far from anywhere and the fact that he faced a long and lonely night on a lumpy mattress with only a thin blanket to cover him. After all, he was a man, and an Italian man at that. Looking back, his reserve was probably the thing that won me over. It endeared him to me even more. And although I still had not admitted it to myself, he was becoming very dear to me indeed. So when I took a cup of tea into his bedroom the next morning, and set it down on the old plastic chair beside him, I was taken aback when he stretched out an arm from under the blanket and took my hand in his. His hand was very cold, and maybe that's why he drew me down to him. The need for some human warmth. But that's not what it seemed like. Not at all. It just felt absolutely right.

The telephone engineers were decidedly bad tempered when they finally arrived much later that morning. There were two of them and the younger one was particularly irritable.

"Why did they have to send us out to do this job? Why did the other crew get the easy job of going to Terni?" He muttered under his breath, cursing as he pulled a broken drill shaft from the huge industrial machine he was using to make a hole through the sitting room wall. It was the second piece he had broken that morning.

"*Porco Dio*! No offence *Signorina*, but these old houses are built like bastions. It's impossible to drill through walls as thick as these. I'm afraid there's nothing we can do. You can't put a phone line in a house like this."

My face must have fallen. I had been looking forward to having a phone line with childlike excitement. It was ridiculous really when having a phone was something I had always taken for granted. But here it had taken on a burning significance. How disappointing to have to give up now.

"Having this phone line means a great deal to the *signorina*. Couldn't you try again?" I heard Mario's voice behind me. He must have walked in just as the workmen delivered their depressing verdict. He had gone out an hour or so earlier to get, as he put it, some urgent supplies.

"Look, I've just bought some fresh bread and *mortadella*. And a bottle of very good wine from Montefalco. Why don't you have a break and we'll try and work out a way of getting this job done?"

The two men didn't take much persuading, and the food, wine and Mario's good-natured humour soon won them over.

"Don't worry *Signorina*. I'll find a way of putting this phone in if it's the last thing I do," said the older workman, wiping the crumbs from his mouth and taking a last slug of wine. "You can't live all by yourself in an isolated place like this without a phone. Anything could happen to you."

It took three more hours, endless volleys of expletives and two more drill pieces before the workmen finally succeeded in making a small hole through the three-foot thick stone wall. They looked almost as happy as I was and the older one grabbed his younger colleague by the waist and they did a little dance to celebrate. Mario grabbed me and we did a twirl too, before he kissed me lightly on the hand and made a small bow.

"So what happens now? When do I get my phone?" I said, just like a small child.

"Take it easy *Signorina*. First we have to hook the wire up outside to the main telephone line. Then we have to run a test to see if it works. And then we have to fit your handset. Here, I've brought one with me for you." He opened a brown box to reveal an ancient looking grey telephone, the same one I had seen in the *carabinieri's* office. "Let's say, by the end of the week you should be all fixed up."

"The end of the week?"

"No chance of getting it all finished today?" I was discovering that Mario could be very persuasive. "I'd feel much happier about leaving my girlfriend all alone here if I knew I could speak to her by phone. Unfortunately, I have to leave tomorrow."

"Oh if you put it like that. Come on Luigi, let's get to work again." The older workman slapped his younger colleague on the back. "You can see they're in love and we must do our bit to see that they aren't kept apart. Where's your sense of romance?"

Looking back, the twenty four hours that followed were some of the happiest of my life. Or perhaps the feeling of heady contentment was simply heightened by the contrast with the loneliness that had gone before. Mario had bought enough supplies to put together a very passable dinner, based on pecorino sheep's cheese, *salame* and a *frittata*, an omelette filled with pieces of bacon and potato. There was bread for *bruschetta,* which Mario topped with finely chopped piece of tomato. He opened another bottle of red wine, from the Colli Amerini near Narni this time.

"It's not bad, but you wait till you try the wines from the area where I come from". Mario held up his glass and sniffed the wine inside it. "We are very spoilt in Campania. There are excellent white wines, such as *Greco del Tufo* or *Fiano di Avellino.* And the reds are much stronger and bolder than the ones you get up here. One of the best ones comes from a vine that grows on the slopes of Vesuvius. But there are plenty of others as well. I'll bring a couple up next weekend." Next weekend seemed a long way off, but it was gratifying that Mario was already taking it for granted that he would be back. Meanwhile, I was enjoying this one. Every minute.

While Mario made the *frittata*, I made my first two calls with my new phone. First to Charles and then to Jamie. It seemed strange talking to them from the sitting room of my house in San Massano. The line crackled and there was an annoying echo when I spoke to Jamie, but it was good to hear their voices and I could sense the relief in both of them as I told them how things were going and about my job in Rome. I decided not to mention Mario. Who could tell how long it would last?

Later that evening, with mock ceremony, Mario saluted his

comfortless spare room and moved his few things into what he called the Master Suite.

"We'd better get an early night," he said, pulling me gently into the room. "Tomorrow I'm going to thrash you at tennis. And you're going to have to buy me lunch."

"You don't mean you brought your racquet?"

"I said I would, didn't I? Don't tell me you want to chicken out?"

"Certainly not." I had my own racquet somewhere. "Though goodness knows where we'll find a court to play on around here, especially at this time of year."

Finding a court was indeed no easy matter, and we drove from village to village, asking in bars and being directed to courts that were closed for the winter, or had no nets. It was an unusually warm winter day, with a clear blue sky and the softest breeze was wafting wood smoke from the hearths of the stone houses in the villages where we stopped.

"We can't give up," I said. "It's such a perfect day. I know the place that man was telling us about in the last bar we went to. It's on the edge of Lavena. I've never noticed a court there before, but let's go and see."

The court was partly hidden behind a crumbling wall covered with ivy. The lines were barely visible and the net sagged way below the normal height, but it would have to do and we climbed over the broken wire fencing and got out our racquets and balls.

Mario was a good player, with strong measured strokes. He was a natural sportsman, moving around the court with grace and balance. But I was determined to beat him and attacked the ball with aggression.

"Wow," he said, as we sat over lunch a couple of hours later. "You really can play. I'll have to get in some practice if I'm going to beat you." We had gone to a little restaurant that I had never seen before, following a sign that led off the main road onto a small unpaved track. The building was nestled in a cluster of trees and, with its wooden shutters and heart-shaped stencils, it looked like something out of a fairy tale. Inside it was packed, with families and couples sitting down to the ritual of Sunday lunch. We took the last free table.

"I like this place. I think it should become our regular lunch spot after tennis," said Mario, picking up the menu and studying a surprisingly long wine list. He turned to the waitress and ordered a bottle of red wine.

"Seeing that I'm paying this time, I've chosen rather a good bottle from Sicily. I think you'll like it."

The purplish wine splashed into the deep goblets that the waitress had fetched from a cabinet.

"Very good indeed," I said, taking a sip.

"Don't get used to it. Next time you can choose, and you'll be paying too, as I have every intention of getting my revenge."

I watched Mario leave later that afternoon, and wondered, for the hundredth time, what I was letting myself in for. He was on the rebound, and so, to some extent, was I. In any case, there could be no future in a relationship with someone who lived so far away and this was certainly not the right time for a fling. What would George say when he came back at Christmas? What about Angela and Ercolino? Maybe Mario wouldn't come back after all. Perhaps that would be for the best.

The first part of the week flew by and there was little time to brood over what I was increasingly convinced was a rash liaison. On Monday and Tuesday I was due in Rome to work a shift on the newspaper, though I decided to take the train this time. The memory of the fines, and Ercolino's admonishments, was still raw. On Wednesday, I had articles to write for several newspapers in the USA. A newspaper from Sydney had also been in touch. If things carried on like this I would be needing a secretary. Not having to make the trip to Tito's shop saved me a great deal of time. With my new phone, I now had the luxury of sending stories when I wanted, though it was a shame not to have my daily encounters with the friendly shopkeeper. I promised myself that I would go up and see him later, and buy something from his store.

On Wednesday evening, the phone rang. I still couldn't get used to the sound of its shrill ring, breaking through the silence. It was Mario.

"*Pronto.* I've caught you in at last. Where have you been? Living it up in Rome I suppose."

It suddenly struck me how attractive his voice was, quite deep with a slight catch in it. I hadn't really noticed before. It was half an hour before he rang off, promising to call again before he drove up on Friday.

"So you're coming?" It slipped out before I could stop myself.

"Wild horses wouldn't stop me. I'll be there for dinner, and it's your turn to cook."

The long phone conversation had made me late for Tito, but I didn't care, and I still might catch him anyhow. Nothing could dampen my high spirits this evening. I almost fell over the figure sitting at the bottom of my stone stairs. It stood up and turned towards me and I recognised the face as that of Pietro, Caterina's eldest son by a man she met before she married Benedetto. Pietro didn't live at home any more, but I had seen him up in the village a few times when he was visiting his mother. He looked as if he was in his early twenties and he had some of the saddest eyes I had ever seen, though he tried to smile and held out his hand.

"I hope you don't mind *Signorina*, but I needed to see you."

"I don't mind at all Pietro. Have you been sitting here long?"

"I was trying to pluck up the courage. You see, I have to ask you a very big favour, and you're the only one who can help me."

"What is it Pietro? Of course I'll help if I can."

Pietro spilled out his sorry story. How he had been arrested by police in Terni for stealing a moped, and how he was due in court the day after next. It wasn't the first time he had been in trouble and if he didn't find three million lire to stand bail, he would almost certainly be taken into custody.

I did some quick arithmetic. That was almost 1500 pounds.

"That's a lot of money Pietro."

"I know. But you'll get it back. It's just a guarantee for the court. Please *Signorina*, help me. I'll never steal anything again. I don't want to go to prison."

If I cashed in most of the cheques sent by newspapers in recent weeks, I could find the money for him. I didn't have the heart to make him go to jail.

"All right Pietro. I'll help you. But it will take me some time to get the money from the bank. Come back tomorrow evening at about this time."

By now, I should have known that news travelled at lightning speed in these parts, but it still came as a shock when Tito whispered in a confidential tone:

"I see you have found some company *Signorina*." I had just caught him before he closed the shop and he was wrapping up the bread I didn't really want and pouring a few spoonfuls of grated parmesan cheese into a brown paper cone. I didn't know what else to buy.

"May I say I'm delighted that you've found a man." He made it sound rather desperate. "Let's hope that it turns out to be as good a match as that between me and Clara."

Benedetto was waiting for me outside the shop. He wanted to talk about some other news — my encounter with Pietro.

"I know you mean well *Signorina*, but I just had to warn you," he said, playing with the stump of his missing finger on his left hand. "If you give that money to Pietro, you can be sure you'll never see it again. You see he's a drug addict. It's heroin, and he'll do anything to get it. It's very sad, but that money would never get as far as the court. That was a story he made up for you. He's done it before to others."

I felt dreadful telling Pietro that I had changed my mind when he came to collect the money the following evening. His sad eyes filled with tears, but I couldn't afford to lose such a sum and I didn't want to see my hard-earned cash being used to buy drugs. Mario told me that I had no choice when he phoned me later that evening, and we talked over the dilemma at some length. It was reassuring to have someone to discuss things with after all this time.

Mario had brought a lemon tree for me to plant in my garden.

"A touch of the South," he said, hauling it out of the back of his car when he arrived on the Friday evening after work. "That way you'll always think of me when you see it."

If this was courtship Italian style, then I was beginning to like it. Mario was far more romantic than any English boyfriend I had ever had. With every visit, there was some sort of a present. One weekend he brought a box of oranges and squeezed a glass of fresh juice for my breakfast next morning, served on a chopping board as a tray, with a jug of tiny wild cyclamen that he had picked from the woods behind the house.

The two days spent with Mario quickly became the highlight of my week. He never missed a weekend, even though it was a long drive there and back and it meant he hardly ever saw his friends back home. We settled into a pattern, with trips to the lake or walks with picnics to abandoned hill villages on the Saturday and tennis on the Sunday, before lunch at the fairy tale *trattoria*. He had managed to win a couple of times. He was clearly very pleased with his victory, and to be honest, so was I.

I had known for some time that it couldn't last forever. But it was still a shock when it happened. I saw my whole world dissolving before my eyes. Perhaps I had put too much into it, set too much store by something that wasn't entirely under my control. But it had become just that. My entire world. And the thought of losing it made my heart contract. I could actually feel it being squeezed inside my ribcage as I fought to take in the news. It probably didn't help that the bearer of the bad tidings was the foul-mouthed boy from the village.

"*Signorina*, I've just heard some news and I don't think you're going to like it. Someone's bought the bottom part of your house. Some English git. He looks a right tosser if you ask me. I saw him down in Lavena with that agent and I heard them talking. He's due to sign the contract in two days' time. If I were you, I'd get a ruddy move on."

Chapter Seven

"*Porco Dio*. It's bad enough having one English person living in the village. We certainly don't want another one." Ercolino's attempt at a joke fell dismally flat.

"It's not the right moment," whispered Angela to her husband. "Be serious. We need to come up with a plan."

"Sorry. I was just trying to relieve the tension."

Seated around the table were Ercolino, Angela, Cesare, Mirella, George and I. The American was back to put the final touches to his wedding arrangements. He and Asa were due to be married in ten days' time and the immediate members of both families would be assembling soon from Oklahoma and Stockholm.

Mario was not there. He had been forced to leave for Naples late the previous evening, ready for work on Monday morning. I felt very alone as I watched his car reverse with its usual speed down the drive.

"I wish I didn't have to leave you like this," he had said as he kissed me goodbye. He stroked my hair and lifted my chin for a final kiss. "There must be some way we can stop the sale from going through."

But how? Mirella's contacts through a colleague at the agency handling the sale had told her that there was no chance of the buyer backing out.

"He's flying out tomorrow and the appointment to sign the contract with the notary is scheduled for the day after." Sitting at Angela's kitchen table in Terni, where the emergency meeting was being held, Mirella had already worked her way through the best part of a packet of M&S cigarettes. She raised her hands in a gesture of helplessness. "This man seems very determined. Apparently he wants to plant fruit trees on the land and start a small business."

I hung my head at the thought of it. That land was all around my house. It would mean the end of my peaceful haven. The end of my dream.

"There's only one thing to be done," said Cesare, laying his huge hands flat on the formica surface. "We'll just have to get there first."

"How on earth are we going to manage that? You can't just barge into the notary's office." Ercolino was getting worked up.

"I know the *notaio* quite well. He's Baloo for the younger scout group." Was there anyone Cesare didn't know around here?

"I'll talk to him this morning. I'm sure I can make him see reason, and let us in half an hour before this Englishman gets here."

"But what about the money?" I had not spoken until now, but the glimmer of fresh hope stirred me from my torpor.

"Yes, you've got a point. We'll need to get the money together somehow, and have it ready on the table. At least a sizeable deposit."

"We can all chip in something. I'll be the first." George stood up to get his wallet out of his back pocket and fished out several crisp one hundred thousand lire notes. "The Colonel's family is always very generous to me," he said.

"First things first." Cesare stood up and moved towards the door. "I need to call the *notaio* and make him understand that if he wants to carry the flag at this year's Jamboree, he'd better do as I say."

"Do you remember the time we all had a whip around to get you the deposit so you could buy the bottom part of your house? Where in the world will you find friends like that?"

We were in Ercolino's car now and I glanced up at the old house for the last time. He started the Cinquecento and pointed it down the drive. Angela reached forward from the back seat and clutched my hand.

"You will ring me sometimes won't you? You won't just disappear?"

★★★

Driving back through the country lanes to San Massano, I thought hard about how I could get hold of the money I would need to buy the lower half of the house. Always assuming that by some miracle I could manage to get the owners to sell it to me. According to Mirella's contact at the rival estate agency, the agreed price was 18 million lire. That was nearly nine thousand pounds in English money, and I'd need a bit more to pay the notary's fee. Suddenly I realised I was starving. I had been so taken up with the news of the mystery buyer that I hadn't thought about eating since the previous evening.

I drove through Lavena, but there was no time to stop just now. The billboard outside the newspaper shop caught my eye as I passed

"Hunter killed in shooting accident. Local man."

I still had a few hundred pounds in the form of cheques from various newspapers. Thank goodness I hadn't given in to Pietro, though I still felt guilty at the thought of him in prison.

That left a shortfall of several thousand pounds. I really needed to find about ten thousand to be on the safe side. Where could I possibly get hold of that kind of money?

There was a small crowd of people at the bottom of the drive when I turned the last corner on the narrow road to San Massano. Several cars were parked in a row. The group was making its way slowly up to Primo's house. Some of the women were carrying a single flower, and several of them were crying. I recognised Agostino, his head bowed and his mood unusually sombre.

"Oh *Signorina*. What a pleasure to see you, but how sad that it has to be on an occasion like this."

"What's happened Agostino? And what are all these people doing here? Is something wrong?"

"It's Primo." Agostino's voice caught with emotion and he held his hand to his mouth. "He's dead. Shot while out hunting this morning. Someone must have heard him move and mistaken him for a wild boar."

"How absolutely dreadful." I couldn't think of anything else to say. "Poor poor Nadia."

"He was my second cousin. We used to play together as kids, before he went away to Rome." Agostino drew a clean blue cotton handkerchief from the pocket of his moleskin trousers and wiped his eyes. "Here, you'd better come up too and pay your respects. After all, he was you next door neighbour."

Before I could say anything, Agostino had linked his arm with mine and was guiding me up the path to Primo and Nadia's dark pink front door. There was no need to use the shiny brass knocker. The door was already ajar and a stout woman in a dark skirt and top opened it further to let us in.

"Buongiorno Agostino. Buongiorno *Signorina*." It was Adele, Primo's younger sister. "Thank you for coming. He's…he's over there."

She pointed in the direction of a bedroom, where, to my horror, I saw an open coffin propped up on stilts. Nadia was sitting by the side of it, dressed in dark purple, mascara streaking her face. Around her, a huddle of women sobbed and prayed. Word must have spread fast, and soon, a seemingly interminable procession of friends and relatives arrived, each time signalling a new bout of crying and despair. For the first ten minutes or so, I sobbed with the rest of them. Primo had been a good man and it really was very sad and shocking to see him lying lifeless in a coffin, though I tried hard not to look. But as time wore on I started to wonder how I could make an exit, without causing offence. All the other visitors seemed to be settling in for the rest of the day. I was beginning to feel quite faint and looked around earnestly to see if anyone had though to put out a few sandwiches. I'd even settle for a biscuit, or some of those boiled sweets Italians always have sitting around in silver bowls on their coffee tables. Incredibly in a country where eating seemed to take up a good part of most people's time and thoughts, there was not a crust of bread in sight.

It was hard to take in how quickly everything had happened and the speed with which poor Primo was being dispatched. It was only yesterday that I had seen him feeding his beloved hunting dogs and oiling his gun ready for the next day. Now he was dead and within just over six hours of breathing his last, his family had somehow found the time to notify all his friends and acquaintances, organise several huge wreaths made out of gladioli and palm leaves, arrange to have black edged posters stuck on walls and lampposts throughout San Massano and neighbouring villages, order a coffin lined with lilac coloured satin, book the priest and the church for the funeral the next day, and move heaven and earth to secure a place for him in the local cemetery.

As soon as I could decently take my leave, I extricated myself from the sad wake and walked slowly up the drive to my own house. It might have been heartless, but I urgently needed to eat something. And I needed to make an important phone call to my building society in Brighton. Sitting among the distraught relatives next door had given me time to think. Perhaps I could take out a second mortgage. Goodness knows how I would pay it back, but this was an emergency.

Less than an hour later, both missions had been successfully accomplished. Between bites from a giant *panino* made from a hunk of bread and some left over *prosciutto crudo*, I fished out my address book and found the telephone number that I needed. After a short discussion with a secretary I was put through to the manager. My story was well rehearsed. I needed the money to carry out repairs on my house in Brighton. The window frames were in urgent need of replacement.

"So how much would you need?"

"I should say about ten thousand pounds."

"That shouldn't be a problem. I'll get my secretary to put the forms in the post and you should have the funds transferred to your account by the end of next week."

There was more good news when Ercolino telephoned me a few hours later. Having a phone had really changed my life. Cesare had managed to persuade the notary to see us half an hour before the appointment with the Englishman. And he had also promised to make sure that the owners of the lower part of my house were there early too. The meeting was fixed for the following day at noon.

"We're coming up to San Massano this evening anyway," said Ercolino. "So maybe you'd like to come round and have dinner with us. There's something I want to say to you."

An invitation to dinner with Angela and Ercolino was something that I always looked forward to. Partly for the food, for it would be hard to say which of the pair was the better cook. Angela made the best spaghetti with clams that I had ever tasted anywhere, and Ercolino could turn his hand to a rich array of peasant dishes, all of them delicious – beans casseroled with garlic and tomato sauce, lentils cooked with tiny shreds of cured ham and my favourite, *panzanella* – chunks of stale bread doused with olive oil and topped with fresh tomatoes and basil. But the company was the main attraction. Angela and Ercolino always had a story to tell, about their whirlwind romance in Liverpool or their elopement to Sweden. Angela's father, now in his seventies, had still not forgiven her for marrying a poor Catholic boy, and a Communist at that. She and Ercolino had gone back to England just once, to see her two sisters and a few old friends, but Angela's father had refused to see them.

"I won't go back again, not unless my father changes his mind." In all the years, Angela had never given up hope.

"I certainly won't be going back there in a hurry." Ercolino put a dish of *panzanella* on the table. "Orrible food and freezin' cold weather. I remember it was August when we went and her sister had to switch the central heating on for me. I've never been so cold in my life."

I opened the bottle of red wine that I had brought with me and poured a glass for all of us.

"What is it that you wanted to talk to me about?"

"Have something to eat first. You see I made your favourite *panzanella*?"

Angela was shifting uncomfortably in her chair.

"Go on Ercolino. Say what you've got to say. Then we can all get on with the rest of the evening."

He cleared his throat.

"You know you are like a daughter to us don't you?"

He took a long sip of his wine and tried again.

"The thing is, we don't want to see you get hurt."

I waited patiently for him to explain.

"I know I told you to go and find a boyfriend, but I didn't mean one from down South," he blurted out.

"What are you saying?"

"I'm just sayin' that of all the boys you could have found, you had to go and choose one from bloody Naples."

"Whatever is the problem with that?" I took a big sip of wine myself now. I was very fond of Ercolino, but sometimes he really could be extremely irritating.

"Well I'm not saying he's a *camorrista* or anything like that. I'm sure he's a very nice boy and I know he comes from a good family." Another long pause. "It's just that down there, the men have a dreadful reputation for being *gigolos*. Especially with foreign girls. The chances are he's already seeing someone else when you're not around. How do you know what he gets up to during the week?"

When Mario telephoned later that evening for our nightly chat I carefully avoided mentioning anything about what Ercolino had said to me. We talked about poor Primo and I confessed that I had had to escape the grieving to get something to eat.

"It's strange no one eats," I said. "Where I come from it's considered only right and proper to send your loved ones off with a bit of a party."

Mario laughed. "In Italy, grief is such an overwhelming emotion that it makes eating impossible. It's considered very bad form to show any desire for food or drink, so it's just as well you didn't ask for anything."

We talked about the next day's appointment at the notary, and the chances of persuading the owners to sell the property to me instead of the Englishman.

"At the end of the day, it will probably all come down to money," he said. "Why don't you offer a bit more? That usually works."

"I wish you were going to be here to help me out." Even I was surprised by the comment. I couldn't remember the last time I'd made such a blatant admission of need.

"I wish I could too. But I can't take time off work at such short notice. I'll ring you tomorrow to see how it's gone. And we'll talk things over properly when I come up on Friday."

I couldn't have wished for greater support in my ordeal at the notary's office. George drove me down to Terni, dropping off his fiancée Asa and her sister in the high street on the way, so that they could go shopping for the big day. Asa had brought her wedding dress with her from Sweden but she still needed a few final touches to her outfit. One important item on the list was her bridal lingerie.

"I thought I'd buy that here in Italy," she said, turning round from the front seat. Her sister, who was seated next to me, giggled. "I'm sure we can find something that George will like."

Angela and Ercolino were waiting for us outside the notary's studio. I noticed that Ercolino was looking unusually smart in a checked shirt and dark blue jacket. Cesare and Mirella were already inside, talking to the notary. Seated on a row of chairs against one wall was a group of people who were unmistakably related. I recognised the father and son immediately as the pair who had threatened me in San Massano. There were two other men, who judging by their teeth and orange hair, must surely be the father's brothers. A woman seated between them had slightly thicker hair, which she had had the sense to dye, though perhaps she could have opted for something other than a dirty blond colour. Her teeth, however, condemned her instantly as the three men's sister. All five of them glowered in my direction.

"What's she doing here? I thought the deal was with a man," said the father. He was as rude and surly as I remembered him.

"Yeah, who asked her to come?" The son spoke with the same gormless voice as his father.

"Now, if you wouldn't mind being quiet for a moment, I'd like to explain something to all of you." The notary sat at his finely polished desk and methodically rearranged the dark green leather blotter and a solid silver letter opener. "There's been a slight change of plan," he went on calmly. "This lady here," and he gestured in my direction, "has decided that she would like to buy the property, so I suggest that we all come to a mutual agreement and proceed with the sale without further ado."

"Over my dead body. I'm not selling our beloved father's house to the likes of her. Let's not forget that she's done everything possible in the last few weeks to put off any buyers who came to see the place." The orange-haired father stood up and jabbed a yellow-stained finger angrily in my direction.

This was too much for Cesare.

"Sit down," he boomed. "And show a little respect for a lady, who is, after all, a guest in our country."

The man sat down abruptly, still muttering under his breath. Cesare glared at him.

"And may I remind you that various members of this family have used menaces to try and convince this lady to part with money. I personally consider this the shabbiest form of behaviour and will not hesitate to report it to my good friend the chief of police should it prove necessary."

"Hear hear. I say we go to the police right now." Ercolino was up on his feet now, red faced and jumping up and down with anger. Cesare placed a calming hand on his friend's arm and drew him back into his seat.

George was not to be outdone. After all, he was an actor.

"I am quite sure that these good people meant no harm when they came to San Massano that day." He spoke Italian with a strong American accent, but his delivery was flawless. "And I am equally sure that they will see the justice in letting this lady have the chance to buy the property so close to the part she already occupies, and which she loves and treasures so dearly."

The notary looked at his watch and coughed.

"Under Italian law, there is a legal requirement to offer a property to the nearest neighbour before selling it to a third party," said the notary. The five family members exchanged astonished glances. "So I have the papers all ready here to sign. You can put a cross if it is easier." The notary looked at the oldest brother and hurriedly withdrew the expensive fountain pen he had been proffering, replacing it with a cheap biro.

"What about the price then? I say we should ask for more if she wants it so much."

"The price will remain the same, that is to say eighteen

million lire," thundered Cesare. "That's unless you'd like to come and discuss the matter with me and my friend the chief of police?"

"No no, that won't be necessary." It was the sister who spoke, for the first time since the meeting began. "Come on, let's sign and get out of here. And Aldo, just be quiet for once in your life. You've done enough damage as it is."

Ten minutes, and what seemed like several dozen signatures later, the notary placed the documents in three neat piles and applied his heavily embossed stamp to the top page of each of them.

"Now, if you will just release the deposit, we can consider the whole procedure concluded."

Cesare drew out an envelope and handed it over.

"I think you'll find that there is one million lire, plus your own fee of five hundred thousand lire." The notary took the envelope and counted out the contents carefully.

"Splendid. The balance of seventeen million lire needs to be paid within fourteen days or the contract is null and void. I wish you all a pleasant afternoon." He turned to shake the hand of each person in the room.

Outside in the waiting room, raised voices could be heard.

"What do you mean I'm too late? I've come here specially!" A fair haired man in his thirties, a holdall at his feet, was remonstrating in English with the secretary, who clearly understood very little, other than that the man was extremely angry.

"You know what they say," said Ercolino, unable to hide the smile on his face as the notary hastily ushered us out of his office. "The hearly bird catches the worm!"

George insisted on taking us all to his favourite bar in Piazza Tacito, where he ordered a bottle of prosecco to celebrate. A slim young woman with a cascade of long dark black hair brought an ice bucket with the bottle to our table.

"Giorgio. What a lovely surprise. How are you?" She leant over and gave him a kiss on each cheek.

"Fine thanks Loredana. You look in great shape." Was it my imagination, or had he coloured slightly in the face? He opened the bottle and poured a glass for all of us. Loredana stood by with her tray under one arm, smiling.

"Here's to the hearly birds," said George, raising his glass.

Ercolino touched his glass to George's, and said pointedly:

"Yes George, and here's to your wedding. Only just over a week to go."

I raised my glass and smiled at my friends. For they really were the most extraordinarily good friends, and I knew I was very lucky to have them.

"Thank you all of you. Thank you so much. I promise you'll get your money back very soon."

But somewhere in the back of my mind there was an uneasy feeling. Why did I always have to be on my own? And where was Mario when I needed him?

George and I picked up Asa and her sister by the main shopping area before heading back to San Massano. Judging by the amount of bags and packages they had with them, it had been a busy morning.

"We found some darling shoes for my going away outfit," Asa whispered to me. She bundled some of the bags into the rear seat next to me. There was no more room in the boot. "And some very fetching suspenders and stockings to wear under my wedding dress!"

She was a pretty girl, though not as stunning as some of the women George had been out with. Somewhat tactlessly in my opinion, he kept photographs of several of his ex-girlfriends in his sitting room. Asa was friendly and gentle, and I was beginning to like her. She was also clearly very much in love.

"Come on you girls. Stop gossiping and let's get back. I need to go and see Pops. He'll be wondering where I am. I promised I'd sit and watch his favourite General Patton movie with him this afternoon."

"Again!"

Like most of George's women, Asa was less than enthusiastic about George's devotion to the Colonel.

"He likes it. And I like to keep him happy." George had picked up speed now. "Anyway, we've got to look after the golden goose. Who do you think paid for all the packages you just bought?"

Tito and Clara's wedding was a strangely moving affair. It was held on a Thursday. It was traditional for grocery store owners in Italy to marry on a Thursday. Something to do with closing times, though the only time Tito had ever closed his shop was the day he drove over the mountain pass to ask for Clara's hand. The whole village had been invited to the wedding, including me. I couldn't help wishing that Mario had been there too. The ceremony was held in the tiny frescoed church set right on the crest of San Massano. Tito walked the short distance from his house, helping his old father to negotiate the steep path up the hill to the church door. When the bride arrived, ten minutes later on the arm of her older brother, a round of spontaneous applause broke out from the church pews. Clara was dressed in a knee length cream coloured suit, with fur trimming on the neck and wrists. Her hair was cut short and she wore no covering on her head. A shy smile etched on her face, she walked the few paces to the front of the church where Tito and Don Gaetano were waiting for her. Her brother released her arm gently and took his place in the front pew with the rest of Clara's family. Both bride and groom stumbled on their vows and Don Gaetano patiently made them repeat the oaths.

"Till death do us part."

"Till death do us part."

I looked round and saw that almost all the women had handkerchiefs out and were dabbing at their eyes. Even though some of the villagers complained about the prices Tito charged, everyone liked the shopkeeper and was glad that he had at last found such a gentle soul with whom to share his life.

"Now for the best part. We can finally go and eat." Agostino, who was sitting next to me, had been fidgeting on the hard bench since the service began.

"Come on *Signorina*. Let's go and see what kind of spread Tito's put on for us. With him married, that means that you and I are the only ones left without a spouse!"

Mario arrived on Friday as usual, and I instantly forgave him for his absence earlier in the week. He brought me flowers, and a big polyester box which I opened to reveal four fat mozzarella cheese balls, sitting in a milky liquid.

"They're made of buffalo milk. You can see the buffalo grazing in the fields between Naples and Rome. The mozzarella is far better than anything you'll taste anywhere else."

He was right. The cheese had a tangier flavour than any mozzarella I had ever tasted. With it we ate a soft bread with salt in it, bought from a bakery just near where Mario lived. And *friarelle,* which I had never seen before.

"They're a sort of local leafy vegetable which you boil and drain and then simmer in olive oil, garlic and chilli pepper. It only grows in the Naples area."

"Divine. I bet Angela and Ercolino would like these."

"Why don't we invite them next weekend? I can bring all the ingredients and cook them a real Neapolitan dinner."

So we were already talking about next weekend. The thought cast a pall on the rest of the evening. I'd never been in a long distance relationship before and I was finding it hard to get used to it. What was supposed to happen between Monday and Friday?

Perhaps it was my mood that evening that paved the way for what happened the following day. Whatever the cause, the events ruined the rest of the weekend, and sounded an ominous warning about what very different people Mario and I really were. We were driving back to San Massano after an evening in a *trattoria* near Montecupo when it happened. All of a sudden, a giant silhouette loomed out of the darkness, followed by a deafening thump and a sinister sensation as flesh collided with metal. The car shuddered to a halt, and through what was left of the windshield, smoke pouring out of the engine, we managed to discern the cause of the impact – one very large and now badly wounded wild boar. The windscreen had shattered into a thousand pieces and the passenger door had been completely crumpled and jammed tight by the weight of the poor beast. After checking that neither of us was hurt, my first thought was to tend to the injured animal. I climbed over into the back and opened the door to see the massive form lying on the side of the road. The animal's head and chest were streaked with blood and a faint rasping sound suggested it was now beyond help. The wild boar was clearly dying. I looked around for some heavy instrument to put it out of its misery and picked up a huge spanner that I found in the boot. It was only afterwards that people who know more about wild boar than I do pointed out that trying to clout such a fierce animal over the head, however moribund it might appear to be, was pure folly.

I cursed Mario for not helping me to finish the boar off. He meanwhile, was uttering a barrage of expletives and pointing to the rising cloud of steam.

"Look what it's done. That will cost a fortune to put right."

151

Mario threw his keys on the ground furiously. I had never seen him angry before.

Not only had one side of the car been caved in and most of the front badly damaged, but steam was escaping from the radiator. It was now one o'clock in the morning, and we were stranded, miles from anywhere, with not another soul in sight. Or so we thought.

Suddenly, as if out of nowhere, a jeep appeared out of the darkness and pulled up alongside us. What a stroke of luck. Someone had come to our rescue. Without a word, four men climbed out of the jeep and opened the rear door. They quickly spread out a tarpaulin on the immaculate interior before turning to the wretched beast, which had now breathed its last gasp. In a matter of seconds, they had hauled the massive animal into the back of the vehicle, slammed the door and left. We stood there, unable to take it in. They hadn't so much as asked if we were all right, let alone if we minded that they were making off with the cause of all our troubles. And how had they known about the wild boar in the first place?

Much later, our encounter with the wild boar helped me to understand a number of things. First, that when it comes to food, Italians, and country people in particular, are very determined. I subsequently learned that our wild boar would have been worth a small fortune for its steaks, hams and sausages. The second lesson was that no matter how deserted the countryside may seem, there is always someone watching you. Finally, it made me question my whole future with the man who had been in the car with me that night. I could quite understand him being angry about the damage to his car, but that was all he seemed to have cared about. What I couldn't forgive was his ill temper and his indifference to a badly wounded animal. We drove home very slowly in an uncomfortable silence. If I was not very much mistaken, we had just had our first row.

The atmosphere was still tense when I drove Mario to the station on Sunday evening. His car would take several days to repair and the bill would indeed be considerable. Dirty Paolo had given a quote that had made Mario wince when we had called him up to look at the car that morning. The mechanic had shaken my hand politely and behaved impeccably, but the message was all too clear. There would be no discounts for my boyfriend.

"Oh ciao!" I looked over in the direction from where the familiar voice was coming from. "Ciao, over here!" It was Fabrizio.

With him, on the station platform, were his mother Colomba and his father Amato. An old lady who must have been his grandmother, was also in the group. So too was his married sister Daniela, her husband and two children and several younger men and women.

"Meet my cousins," and he introduced them one by one.

"Why are you all here Fabrizio?"

He looked slightly embarrassed.

"They've come to give me the big send-off. I'm leaving to do my military service."

The sound of quiet sobbing interrupted him and we turned to see Colomba rummaging in her large handbag for another handkerchief. Her husband was trying to comfort her, placing a protective arm around her shoulder.

"*Mamma*. I'm only going to Viterbo. It's less than 50 kilometres away."

"It might as well be at the other end of the earth." Colomba was inconsolable at the thought of losing her only son.

"But I'll be back every other weekend. And I'm allowed to phone home once every three days. "

Like me, Colomba and Amato were now the proud owners of a telephone, although they rarely used it.

"Come on *Mamma*. The train will be leaving soon." Fabrizio threw me a sideways glance and whispered.

"Sorry to have got you caught up in all this. Say hello to Melissa for me, won't you?"

"Here's a few things I've packed for you to make sure you don't go hungry." Colomba handed Fabrizio a big wicker basket stuffed with all sorts of packages wrapped in cheesecloth and greaseproof paper.

"And here's a bit of cash just in case you need it." Amato pressed a few notes into Fabrizio's hand. The porter strode down the platform and donned his red peaked cap, a sign that the train was about to leave.

"Goodbye *amore mio*. I'll miss you so dreadfully." Colomba had dissolved into tears again and planted a wet kiss on her son's cheek. The rest of the family, many of the women also crying, embraced Fabrizio. The men patted him affectionately on the back. He climbed the steep step up into the carriage. The guard blew his whistle and the train pulled out.

"*Arrivederci*. Take care. Make sure you eat enough. *Arrivederci!*"

How many times I had stood on this station platform. Saying hello. Saying goodbye. But it had always been arrivederci. Never addio. For I had always been planning to come back, sooner or later. Until this time. This time it was different, and it was one of the hardest goodbyes I had ever endured. This time it was addio. Forever.

★★★

"I suppose I should be heading off too. My train leaves in five minutes. From platform two."

To get to the platform, you had to walk down some steps to the underpass, and come up the other side. I made to walk with him to the staircase.

"No, don't bother. I can go by myself." The coolness between us was still unmistakable.

154

"I'll come with you if you like."

"No, really. It's fine. I'll call you sometime this week."

He turned on his heels and was gone. Sometime this week? That said it all. Mario always called me on a Monday, the minute he got in from work. Things really had taken a turn for the worse.

Deciding what to wear to George's wedding was something I should have done long before. I knew that it was going to be a very grand affair, with a ceremony at the Cathedral in Spoleto and the reception at George's favourite, and extremely expensive restaurant just outside the city walls. I must wear something smart but I didn't know exactly what kind of outfit to buy. Should it be a dress or a skirt? Long or short? And would the women be wearing hats? I decided to go up to George's house in the village to find out more about the dress code. Most of the rest of Asa's family would have arrived by now and someone would be sure to be able to offer me some good advice.

There were indeed a great many people in George's house when I arrived. I recognised Asa's sister, Sara, and called out to her. She turned and managed a thin smile, but she was not her usual friendly self.

She went back to what she had been doing before, massaging the neck and shoulders of a figure seated on a wrought iron chair, speaking softly and kissing the person's head. It was Asa. She looked dreadful, pale, with red rimmed eyes, her blonde hair greasy and dishevelled. Several other people I had never seen before were moving around the room uncomfortably, talking in low voices.

"Has something happened? Where's George?"

"He's in the camper van with the Colonel. You'd better go and see him." Sara went back to massaging Asa's neck.

George was sitting on the couch next to the Colonel when I opened the door of the camper van a few minutes later. The television blared and figures dressed in khaki moved on the screen.

"Go on General. You can do it! Get those tanks and drive those bastards out of the desert!"

The Colonel was watching his favourite scene.

"Oh hi there. Want to come and watch General Patton rout the Germans?" George smiled weakly and moved up a bit to make room for me.

"What's going on George? Why are you in here?" I stepped up and sat down beside him.

"You could say I'm in hiding. I'm trying to avoid Asa's family."

"Why? They all look perfectly nice people to me."

"Yes they are. It's just that they're mad at me. You see, I've called the whole thing off. Yep, right at the very last minute. The guests, the presents, the dress. Everything was ready. You could call it a chronic case of cold feet. The trouble is, I realised that I wasn't absolutely sure I was doing the right thing. And you can't get married if you're not one hundred percent certain. Marriage is for keeps."

Chapter Eight

It was Thursday evening before Mario phoned that week. I tried to make my tone deliberately cool, though my heart missed a beat at the sound of his rich warm voice.

"I'm sorry, but things have been quite hectic here, and it's been difficult getting around without a car."

"Well the garage here should have got it ready by now," I said. I certainly wasn't going down to Dirty Paolo's workshop to check it out.

"I've already looked at the train times and there's one that gets in at seven o'clock tomorrow evening. I could catch that quite easily. That is if you want me to come. And you don't mind driving down to pick me up."

"I'll be there," I promised, as casually as I knew how. "See you tomorrow."

Was he coming back just to pick up his car? Or was he coming back because he wanted to see me? It was impossible to tell. Ercolino's warning was still ringing in my ears. I didn't know what to think. But I did know that I was very much looking forward to seeing Mario again.

That's when you should have brought a stop to the whole thing. Before it went any further. You were still in time to save yourself from getting in any deeper. And getting hurt the way you always knew you would.

I was on the train now, heading for Rome and the long final journey.

"Birra, coca, panini." I waved the young lad and his bucket of refreshments away.

"Cheer up Signorina! It might never happen." He went on his way down the corridor.

How could he possibly know that it already had?

★★★

"Here, I bought these for you at the station. I'm afraid they've wilted a bit in the train." Mario held out a bunch of brightly coloured flowers wrapped in dark purple paper.

"You can consider it a peace offering if you like. Not that I'm really all that sure what I'm supposed to have done."

The tops of some greens sticking out of a large paper carrier bag caught my eye. The *friarelle*. So he hadn't forgotten his promise to cook a Neapolitan dinner for my friends.

"I can't believe you've carted that all the way here on the train." I had to admit that whatever his faults, he was unfailingly generous.

"I said I would, didn't I?" He pulled out a box of mozzarella. And some bread.

"And here are some of my mother's home-made preserved aubergines to go with it. She makes jars and jars of it every autumn. We all have to help. It's a family tradition."

"It's a good job they're not courgettes," I smiled and sniffed the flowers he had bought me. "Or Ercolino would have had a fit."

Later, in the sitting room at San Massano, Mario drew me to him and kissed me. We had stopped at a small *trattoria* just outside Lavena on the way back, and he had insisted on paying the bill.

"So, am I forgiven?"

I kissed him back by way of an answer.

"You had me worried there," he said. "I thought that might have been it."

Ercolino was on his best behaviour the following evening when he and Angela came to dinner. I noticed he was wearing a smart pair of dark brown leather moccasins under his blue trousers. Angela had also taken trouble over her appearance. She had on a sage green silk blouse and matching agate earrings, which perfectly set off her rich auburn hair. As always, I was wearing a pair of jeans and a tee-shirt, my hair tied up in a ponytail. Mario was also wearing jeans, with a soft pale blue polo shirt.

Ercolino kissed me on both cheeks and held out a hand to Mario.

"It's a pleasure to meet you." For some reason, he was speaking in English, but Mario appeared not to notice.

Ercolino turned to me again.

"Here, we've brought you some cake for dessert." An elaborately wrapped box with a huge orange bow revealed what looked like a sponge cake topped with every kind of fruit imaginable.

"By the way, there's bad news from the village." He ran his hands through the few thin hairs that remained on top of his head. "It's Clara. They've found out what the problem is with some chest pains she's been having, and I'm afraid it doesn't look at all good. I just saw Tito before we came here and he looked as if he had seen a ghost."

"Poor Tito. If anything happens to Clara I don't like to think what would happen to him. He'd be lost without her." Angela placed a hand affectionately on that of her husband.

"Yes, and I'd be lost without you too," said Ercolino, giving it a squeeze. "Now that's enough of that. Where's the *aperitivo*? You could die of thirst in this place. And I'm starvin' 'ungry"

Over drinks, Ercolino asked Mario about his family and his job. A bit like a father interviewing his daughter's suitor, I thought, but the two men appeared to be getting along.

"So you live with your mother and your sister?" Ercolino

159

accepted another glass of wine and looked round for something to eat. I passed him a piece of *bruschetta*.

"Yes, my father died when I was sixteen and it was all very quick and unexpected. My sister hasn't married, so she still lives at home too, and we both try to give a bit of a hand to my mother. She's a twin, by the way."

I had heard most of it before, but I listened as Mario told Ercolino and Angela about his life in Naples, his work as a sales executive for an export firm and his strong bond with his cousin, who was the son of his mother's twin sister.

"They live in the apartment next door to ours, so we're always together. We're like brothers really. I can't imagine not having him as my next door neighbour. Then there's my mother's older sister and her family. They live close by, so we see a lot of them too."

What a strange life it must be, living so close to one's relatives, I mused. I loved my brothers dearly, but a weekend under the same roof was usually as much as any of us could stand. I couldn't imagine a life surrounded by my own family, let alone anyone else's, though I knew that many Italian couples lived in an apartment next to their in-laws.

The dinner was a great success and both Angela and Ercolino cleared their plates enthusiastically. They each lit up a cigarette and offered one to Mario.

"No thanks. I'm trying to give up. And I have to play an important tennis match tomorrow morning."

It was the first I had heard of it. So our cosy Sunday routine was back on track. We hadn't played since the weekend before the fateful encounter with the wild boar.

"He's a nice boy. I like him," said Ercolino later that week. I had dropped in at their apartment in Terni on the way to pay the balance at the notary's office. True to his word, the manager of my building society in Brighton had transferred the money into my account. A morning at the bank awaited me, organising the withdrawal of the cash and the transfer into lire. I had allowed two hours for the bank and another hour at the notary's office. There would certainly be more forms to sign and more rubber stamping on the notary's immaculate mahogany desk. But first, I wanted to hear what Ercolino and Angela had thought of Mario.

"He's certainly a very good cook," said Angela. She had been giving Mamma her weekly shower and was looking hot and flustered. "Phew, I can feel the warm weather is on its way again."

"I still think you need to find out what he gets up to during the week. You should go and take a look at how he lives and what he does down in Naples." Ercolino was sipping his mid-morning cup of coffee laced with sambuca.

"Oh Ercolino. You're so suspicious. Have you forgotten that we ran off and got married after just six weeks of meeting each other? I'm sure there's no need to check up on Mario. He seems such a lovely lad."

"The difference is that he's from Naples. In any case, it's always best to see someone on their home ground. That's when you see what kind of a person they really are."

I didn't have to wait long. When Mario telephoned that evening, he had a suggestion to make.

"How about you coming down here one of these weekends, instead of me coming up there?"

"What, to Naples?"

"Yes. It's not as bad as they make out, you know." I could picture him smiling at the other end of the telephone. With those perfect teeth and deep green almond-shaped eyes that changed shape altogether when his face broke into a smile.

"Well where would I stay?"

"You can sleep on the sofa bed in the sitting room here at

my mother's place. It's quite comfortable. And she's looking forward to meeting you."

"All right then. Let's plan it for the weekend after next. This weekend it's the festa down in Montebello. It would be a shame to miss that."

"That sounds a great idea. It's my mother's birthday that weekend. And so of course it's her twin sister's birthday too. There's bound to be some kind of celebration."

The evenings were starting to draw out now. A couple of house martins had built a nest in the eaves right outside my bedroom window and I could hear them chattering busily. It was part of a morning ritual. Soon they would be feeding their young before taking them out for their first flying lessons. From the tree outside the bathroom window, nightingales trilled love songs to each other every evening as dusk slowly stole over the hillsides. When Mario's car scrunched up the potholed drive on Friday soon after eight o'clock, it was still light. I leaned out of the kitchen window to watch him climb out of the driver's seat and stretch himself after the long journey. He reached inside and brought out a bunch of pale cream roses tied with a beige coloured silk bow. In all the months we had known each other, I had never seen him arrive without flowers or some other thoughtful present. He opened the boot and pulled out his holdall, his tennis racquet sticking out of one end.

I shouted down to him:

"I hope you've brought lots of money to pay for lunch on Sunday. I'm going to thrash you and it will cost you dear."

"No way." He smiled to reveal a flash of teeth and brushed his hair out of his eyes. "I've been practising this week. You don't stand a chance."

The festa in Montebello was an important annual appointment. In spite of the traditional animosity between the people of San

Massano and those of the larger village further down the valley, everyone came together on this one occasion to produce a spectacle that was the envy of other hillside towns and villages for miles around, as far away as Perugia. The festa celebrated the history of Montebello and the outlying communities through the ages, from its earliest beginnings as a Bronze Age settlement right up to the present day, with scenes re-enacting the harvest in the fields, and the use of farm machinery to help the villagers cut their hay and pack it into bales. Everyone, young and old, played a role, and the women spent months during the winter evenings sewing the costumes and preparing props for the parade through the main street.

Fabrizio was back for the weekend, on leave from his military service. He was greatly looking forward to the evening, not least because he had managed to land a part as one of the bandits, who hid with their horses behind a clump of trees and burst out at regular intervals, firing pistols with real gunpowder. The felt cap he would be wearing would help to hide his ridiculous army haircut. The other attraction was the prospect of seeing Melissa, and maybe spending a few moments together if he was lucky, and her parents weren't too close. The day before, in the piazza at San Massano, she had whispered to him shyly that her father had reluctantly allowed her to take part in the parade, after Don Gaetano had intervened. She still didn't know precisely what role she was going to be playing, but it was something to do with the scene that depicted the Romans taking over Montebello from the local Umbrian tribe.

Don Gaetano watched the procession from a stage erected to host the local dignitaries. He had a look of satisfaction on his face, though he was careful not to stand too close to the mayor of Montebello, who was a Communist.

A woman, dressed in a long ragged robe, her hair flailing wildly, screamed as a young man I recognised as the local butcher's boy dragged her roughly along the street by a rope tied around her wrists. Preceding the wretched woman was a bishop, clothed in a full length cassock and chanting Latin phrases from a missal that he held open in both hands. A solemn drum beat accompanied the group to a small piazza, where several boys dressed in 16th century costumes were building what looked like a huge bonfire.

"The Holy Father condemns you to burn for the hideous crime of witchcraft. Prepare the flames!" Don Gaetano nodded his approval.

"No. I don't want to die. Please. Let me live!" The woman's blood curdling cries were unnervingly convincing. So too was the bonfire, with clever lighting to give the effect of flames leaping high into the sky and an eerie tape recording of crackling to convey the sound of the blaze.

"Oh look. There's Melissa. I'm not sure her father is going to be very pleased."

Ercolino had managed to get hold of one of the tables that had been set out on one side of the main street. Like any festa worth its name, food featured prominently in the proceedings, and we had already eaten plates of *fettuccine* with tomato sauce and lamb chops with roast potatoes, all off it served on earthenware crockery by waitresses dressed in mediaeval costume. Aside from Ercolino, Angela, Mario and I, George was also part of the small group, together with the Colonel, who was in his wheelchair. Asa and her family had left the day after George had called off the wedding.

"Melissa's father might not like it, but Fabrizio certainly will," observed George drily.

Melissa was at the head of a group of what were clearly slave girls. She was wearing a knee length brown coloured robe, ripped up one side to reveal a long pale coloured thigh. Leather thongs criss-crossed her slim calves from her ankles up to her knees and her waist-length hair was softly plaited and fastened with a piece of the same fabric as her skirt. Walking alongside her was a large bosomed harridan who brandished a whip and intermittently turned to berate her charges and order them to walk faster. The woman's stately shape was strangely familiar. She moved swiftly out of the procession and approached our table.

"Hey, don't you recognise me any of you. It's me, Generosa!" She flashed her incorrigible smile. "They chose me to be in charge of the slave girls instead of Settima. You can't imagine how furious she is!"

Fabrizio could be seen gazing at Melissa from the shadows, tilting back his felt hat in unashamed admiration.

The train journey to Naples seemed to take forever. It was too long a distance to ask of my Fiat 500 and in any case, I was worried that it would get stolen. Ercolino had managed to convince me that I was going to the most dangerous of places.

"Make sure you keep an eye on your handbag the whole time," he said. It was just after lunch on Friday and he had offered to drive me to catch the train. "And whatever you do, don't drink the water!"

The station was buzzing when the train finally drew into Naples several hours later. It was hard to move through the throng of people crowded onto the platform, all of them with bulging bags, shouting to make themselves heard above the tannoy.

With some relief, I spotted Mario making his way towards me. He was wearing a pair of pale green light cotton trousers and a short-sleeved cream coloured polo shirt. I began to regret the jeans and long-sleeved tee-shirt I had worn for the journey. It was far hotter here than in Umbria and I was beginning to feel uncomfortably warm.

"Come on. You look as if you could do with something to drink. "

He steered me out of the station and down a side street

where a small crowd of people stood next to a kiosk festooned with lemons and citrus leaves.

Mario expertly elbowed his way through the throng, a protective arm around my shoulder. His other arm held my holdall.

"How about a fresh lemon soda?" He ordered the drinks and paid as the barman placed two glasses of pale yellow frothing liquid on the counter.

"Drink it down in one, before it stops frothing."

I did as I was told.

"They're real lemons, from Sorrento. Isn't that just the most refreshing drink you've ever tasted?"

The drive back to Mario's mother's apartment was one of the most frightening experiences of my life. Mario gunned his car in and out of the thick traffic, ramming his foot on the accelerator to overtake as soon as there was the slightest opportunity and deftly switching back onto the right side of the road in time to avoid what looked like a certain head-on collision. He turned to look at me and, seeing my pale face, placed a comforting hand on my knee. I swiftly took it off and placed it back on the steering wheel.

"I think you need both hands to drive in this place," I said. "Do you always drive so fast here?"

"You have to, or you'd be stuck sitting in the traffic all day. Relax, you'll get used to it. Look, we're almost there."

I had seen Mount Vesuvius in pictures, but gazing at it across the Bay of Naples was like watching a scene from a film. I half expected Sophia Loren to walk down the street at any moment.

"That's the view from our sitting room window." Mario had miraculously found a space on the busy road and parked the car. He took out my holdall and hoisted it over one shoulder. "It's a bit of a walk up to our apartment. Now you can see why I keep so fit."

Five flights of stairs later, we reached a brown painted front door. An elegantly dressed woman with dark brown hair was waiting to welcome us.

"I heard your voices coming up the stairs. You must be Mario's girlfriend. I'm his mother, Consiglia. Welcome to Naples." She held out a well manicured hand and grasped mine warmly. "Did you have a dreadful journey? You must be very hungry. Come into the kitchen and talk to me while I finish getting dinner ready. My sister and her family will be here soon."

An appetising aroma wafted out from the direction in which Consiglia was heading. The kitchen was small by English standards, but it opened out onto a pretty terrace, with pots of geraniums and basil stacked along the wall. Slices of aubergine were laid out on several tea towels to dry in the sun. Consiglia gathered them up and threw them into a massive frying pan of olive oil. A large saucepan on the next ring of the stove was bubbling with a thick red tomato sauce.

"I thought you'd like to try a *parmigiana di melanzane*. It's a traditional Neapolitan dish." Mario's mother brushed past me to pick a fistful of basil leaves from a terracotta pot. She placed a layer of fried aubergine slices in a deep dish, ladling out some thick sauce on the top, and some chopped *scamorza* smoked cheese on top of that. She strewed a handful of basil leaves and powdered a generous quantity of grated parmesan cheese. Then she repeated the whole process, before placing the dish in the oven and lit the gas with a match.

"While that's doing, we can have our *antipasto*. Come into the dining room. I'm sure I just heard Maria and everyone else arrive. It's going to be a bit of a squeeze. I hope you don't mind."

It was indeed a squeeze as we crammed in around a long table that took up most of the tiny sitting room. As well as Mario's mother and two aunts there was his sister Gisella and a seemingly never-ending array of cousins. I counted sixteen people when we finally sat down to lunch. As a guest, I was given a place of honour near the end of the table, where there was a little more leg room, though not much. Next to me was Consiglia's twin sister Maria, who looked identical apart from a slightly different hairstyle, and, on the other side was her daughter Silvia, a glamorous girl in her mid-twenties with a full mouth, perfectly outlined in a rich red lipstick. All the men were sitting at the other end of the table, with Mario at the head and his closest cousin Lorenzo by his side. Lorenzo was a tall, good-looking young man, a year or two older than Mario. His father, slight, with wire-rimmed glasses and a quiet, gentle manner, sat next to him. He was flanked by Silvia's boyfriend Daniele, a dentist.

"He has a surgery down in town and is doing very well," Maria told me proudly. "They've been courting for seven years now, so I expect he'll propose soon. Such a lovely boy."

The conversation at the women's end of the table revolved around recipes and other domestic topics. As Consiglia served the *parmigiana di melanzane* onto pretty ceramic plates, there was much discussion about what time of year the aubergines were at their best and who sold the tastiest *scamorza*. I suppose I shouldn't have been surprised by now, but the *parmigiana* was just one of a dozen or so dishes that were served as an *antipasto*. The others included fried artichokes, marinated anchovies, squid cooked in olive oil, tiny mozzarella and fritters filled with what turned out to be seaweed.

"I don't suppose you have seaweed fritters in England?" Maria put another two of them on my plate. "What do you eat on a special occasion back home?" Thoughts of my father's magnificent sirloin of roast beef flooded into my mind. He used to spend all Saturday morning browsing the shops to find the best cut of meat before shutting himself off in the kitchen in the evening to prepare what would be a spectacular dinner.

"We eat beef, with roast potatoes and vegetables and a sort of…" How on earth did you explain Yorkshire pudding?

"What, all on the same plate? I don't think I'd like that."

Silvia, the pretty cousin picked up her boyfriend's plate and piled on some more fritters before setting it in front of him. "Eat up *tesoro*. You know how much you love these."

"And what kind of pasta do you have before the meat course?" This time it was Consiglia talking. I couldn't help noticing how elegant she looked, despite having just cooked a massive lunch for sixteen people.

"We don't really eat pasta. Just the beef. Well, maybe with a starter first." The expressions of disbelief made it clear there was no point in trying to explain.

Maria butted in:

"Well, looking on the bright side, I suppose that means less washing up! Come on Consiglia, let's get these plates washed, then we can get the pasta onto the table. Where have you put your rubber gloves?"

The women whisked the plates from the table, gently pushing me back into my chair when I tried to stand up to help them, and chattering cheerfully about techniques for removing encrusted food from plates, they moved into the kitchen.

From the other end of the table, where the men were sitting, came snatches of conversation about cars and football. There was some sort of a big match scheduled for later on that afternoon and the talk was all about the *Napoli* team's chances of moving further up the league.

Several courses later, after pasta with fresh sardines, followed by grilled red mullet, salad and tiramisu, the younger cousins brought in a pot of coffee and a tray of small cream cakes. They were a gift from Silvia's boyfriend.

"What are you going to do now?" Consiglia handed me a cup of espresso and a small plate with a cake that oozed sugary yellow custard. I took the plate politely, wondering if anyone would notice if I didn't eat it.

"Are you going to stay and watch the football match in front of the television with the boys or are you going to come into the kitchen and have a chat with us?"

The match seemed to go on forever, and the cousin in charge of the remote control turned up the volume each time the others yelled out encouragement to their team, or an insult to the referee. From the kitchen came the sound of plates, pots and glasses being stacked, washed and dried, punctuated by peals of laughter and loud conversation. The topic had now turned to the best way of cleaning the cooking hob.

"You have to take out all the burners each time you cook and clean them with bleach before putting them back into the slots," Maria was telling her daughter. "Look, this is how you do it. It's time you learned how to look after a house. You'll have a place of your own one day soon."

Oh not that soon *Mamma*," replied Silvia. "He hasn't even asked me yet. And it'll be at least another three years after that, once we save up for a deposit and buy some furniture."

The women suddenly noticed that I was standing in the doorway and again brushed aside my offer of help. I was rather relieved as dismantling and reassembling a stove didn't sound very appealing. But neither did the prospect of another hour or so of noisy football on the television. My head was beginning to ache from the noise and the feeling of being crammed into a small space with so many people. The warmth of the afternoon was becoming more intense and I moved out on to the small terrace. Shouts from nearby windows, where the same football match appeared to blare out from every apartment, drowned all my thoughts except for one. I had never felt so totally out of place.

Ercolino was right. That should have been another warning. It was all too different from the way my life had been, from the way I wanted it to be.

★★★

170

The conversation, when we finally had it, did not go as I had been expecting. We were in the car on Sunday evening and Mario was driving me to the station to get my train back to Umbria. The rest of the weekend had been clouded by a brooding atmosphere, and although neither of us had said anything, it was clear that something was not right. I had more or less made up my mind that it was not going to work between Mario and I and the sooner we ended it, the better for us both. I resolved to tell him of my decision. Mario had stopped the car next to a small park shaded by towering umbrella pines. Along each side of the road, cars were parked bumper to bumper, their windows shrouded in what looked like black plastic. I was mystified.

"They're bin liners. So no one can see into the cars," said Mario.

"But why?"

He smiled patiently. "We really are from very different worlds aren't we? Where I come from, this is what couples do when they want a bit of privacy together. Sometimes they've been going out with each other for years. There's nowhere else for them to go."

Mario was right about one thing. We really did come from two different worlds and I was beginning to understand that I would never fit in to his.

"I think it's time we faced the truth," I said. "I can't live a life that revolves around a few snatched moments, seeing each other at weekends."

"I couldn't agree more," I waited to see who would have the courage to say the inevitable words that must come next. Him or me?

"That's why I want our relationship to become more full-time." He took my hands in his. "I don't know if this is something that you would like, but I want us to set up home together. I've even asked my boss if I could move away from Naples. Not to San Massano of course, but to Rome, and he's agreed. Why don't we live together and see if it works out?"

171

By now I had missed the train I had planned to catch, but there would be another one in an hour. The sun had started to sink behind the pine trees and several couples had emerged slowly from their cars, removing the bin liners from the windows and holding hands drowsily as they paused for an embrace before going their separate ways.

We too had got out of the car and moved to a wooden park bench to talk over Mario's unexpected plan. You couldn't really call it a proposal. I was still reeling from surprise, just when I had resigned myself to never seeing him again. I still had a great many reservations. But I also realised that I had fallen deeply in love. I told him so, and he told me back. We kissed and hugged each other hard.

"I don't have any bin liners in my car, so we'll just have to wait till next weekend." He pulled me up gently and guided me towards the car.

"Come on, or you'll miss this train too. We'll make some firmer plans when I come up on Friday, and you give it some thought in the meantime. It's not going to be easy for either of us. But I know it's what I want."

"Bloody flies!" Ercolino was perched on the stone steps next to Angela outside their house in San Massano. In his hand was a yellow plastic fly swat, with the corpses of several black flies embedded in the holes. Every often, he slapped it down to kill another one. Angela was fanning herself with a magazine. A few yards away, on an old wooden chair in a corner shaded by the terracotta roofs of the houses, Generosa was surrounded by a halo of white feathers. A plastic bucket was clamped between her legs. Reaching forward to greet her I saw to my horror that she was engrossed in calmly twisting the neck of a cream coloured dove on her lap.

"*Ciao Stella.*" Generosa always called me *Stella*, which meant star. It was her way of showing affection, and disguising the fact that she couldn't pronounce my real name. She held out a grimy hand. It was too late to draw back now.

"I suppose you've come for the funeral. Don Gaetano should be here soon. "What a sad sad business. They waited all that time to find each other, and then she goes and dies after less than a year."

The whole village turned out to say goodbye to Clara. They hadn't known her for very long, but her quiet gracious ways had endeared her to all of them and she always had a bag of sweets to give to the children when they came into the shop.

Tito was deathly white, his eyes sunken into their sockets with grief and his gaze fixed blankly in the middle distance. Next to him, as the procession wound its way on foot behind the coffin and up through the village towards the church was his old father.

"Such a wonderful daughter-in-law. She promised to look after me in my old age." A tear brimmed over each of the old man's red-rimmed eyes.

By the time Mario arrived on Friday evening, there had been time to think over what he had said and start making the first plans. We agreed that Rome would be the most sensible choice, for work and other reasons. It was a half-way point for both of us, so we could come back to San Massano each weekend and Mario would be able to make regular visits to see his mother in Naples.

"And of course, sometimes, she can come and stay with us in Rome," he said lightly.

"Yes. Why not?" I replied vaguely. I hadn't really given the idea much thought.

Finding a flat turned out to be easier than either of us had expected. Mario had bought a copy of *Porta Portese*, a Rome newspaper crammed with small ads that he had picked up at the service station on the way up to San Massano. We pored over the offers at dinner later that evening and I put a squiggle in the margin of three that looked promising. I was due to work a shift at the Rome newspaper on Tuesday, and Mario said he could meet me there afterwards. He would take the day off with the excuse of looking around the new office where he would be working after the move.

The first of the apartments was out of the question. Not far from the Vatican, it was half submerged beneath the pavement of a busy road and had almost no natural light whatsoever. The second one was in a quieter street, but had hideous flock wallpaper and a garish orange plastic sofa in the cramped living room. The last of the three was in a residential part of town out near the Via Appia, an area full of shops and lively markets selling fresh food and flowers. The huge terrace which overlooked a shady park clinched it for both of us. The doctor's wife who owned it, a stylish woman in her forties with long tanned legs, ushered us in to her own much grander apartment next door to sign the contract.

"Sit yourselves down lovebirds and just sign in these three places where I've put a cross. The rent is payable on the fifth day of each month." She paused and adjusted her well-tailored skirt. "I look forward to having you as neighbours."

Settling our respective work issues proved almost as simple. It seemed as if fate was with us. Mario was given a straight transfer to his company's branch in Rome and told he could make a start at the beginning of September. My editor at the newspaper was just as helpful when I dropped by to see him later that day. He said he would be happy to give me as many shifts as I could handle. He also told me that he'd heard the job of correspondent for the Washington Post would soon be up for offer as the present incumbent was planning to go back to the US.

"It's not great money, but it's a name that opens a great many doors," he said. "You should think about putting in for it. I think you'd stand a good chance."

"So let me get this right. You've decided to shack up with the first man you meet without asking anyone's opinion? And a Neapolitan at that!"

Ercolino was working himself up into one of his states and even Angela's powers of persuasion and diplomacy were having little effect in calming him down.

"Be quiet Ercolino. You're not her father. Come on. Let's all have a drink and then I'll get some lunch. It's the heat that's getting to us all. Damn, there's not even any water." She tuned the cold tap on to fill the saucepan for some pasta, but a thin trickle spattered out before stopping altogether.

"*Porco dio!* You're dead right I'm not her father. If I was, I'd have thrown her out by now."

Ercolino turned to me, his face now as red as the shirt he was wearing. "I don't think you realise what you're letting yourself in for. You drive me round the wall."

Normally, Ercolino's mixed metaphors would have made me smile, but this time I was too upset. I mumbled a goodbye and headed for the door, desperate for some fresh air and to be by myself.

Angela was right. The heat was partly to blame. The warm air that had been blowing like a hairdryer for most of the day seemed to be making everyone irritable, even up here in the hills. It didn't bear thinking about what the temperature must be like down in Terni.

Shielding my eyes against the mid-day sun I strode briskly down into the piazza where my Fiat 500 was parked in the baking heat. The steering wheel felt as if it had been plucked from red hot embers. How stupid of me not to have parked in the shade.

"*Signorina*. Take this wet cloth and hold it on the steering wheel for a few moments. If not, you'll burn your pretty hands."

I turned round to see Settima's toothless grin peering in through the window.

"Go on, take it. Then I'll wring it out and give you some more."

She handed me a large rag that she had fished out of a bucket of water next to her feet. It felt deliciously cool and I dampened down the steering wheel. She sloshed her hand into the bucket and pulled it out again to dab some cool water on my wrists and forehead.

"That should make things a bit better now. You have to be careful when it gets as hot as this."

I thanked her and started the engine. I was turning to drive out of the piazza when I caught sight of Generosa hurtling down the path towards us.

"I'll strangle her! Stop that woman. She's stolen all my water to feed her sheep and pigs!"

Settima was clearly the object of the burly woman's anger.

"It's time I was off." And grabbing her bucket, still half full of water, Settima quickly skipped off in the direction of her own small house and slammed the front door behind her.

Chapter Nine

We were due to take possession of the new Rome flat on September 1ˢᵗ and there was much to be done before we could move in. Although it was furnished, with expensive looking heavy Italian wooden chairs and tables and a huge walnut bedstead, we wanted to make some personal touches. So during the scorching weekends of August, when most Italian families were by the sea, Mario and I traipsed round the few shops that were still open in Terni to look for bed linen, towels and all the other paraphernalia that goes with setting up house.

Of course I had already done this once before, back in England when Rob and I had moved into the house in Brighton together. But this time was very different and I soon discovered that I had a great deal to learn.

"Why do you need that?" asked Mario as I put two large bath towels in the shopping trolley.

"So we can dry ourselves of course, when we take a shower."

"Oh, don't worry about me. I use a bathrobe. Here, about this?" And he took out the bath towels and threw in a package containing a yellow towelling bathrobe with black spots.

"It looks rather like a bumble bee." I laughed and he caught my hand.

"Come on. Let's go and look at the crockery. The cups and plates left by the good doctor's wife look as if they have seen better days."

"And we must get some…"

"I know, I know. Some decent glasses."

"You read my mind."

"It's one of the first things I noticed when I came to your house."

"How about these?"

Some long stemmed crystal wine glasses joined the bed linen in the trolley, together with six heavy tumblers that had caught Mario's eye. I had to admit that he had impeccable taste.

Looking for a teapot proved a fruitless search. So too did attempts to find a kettle. The few Italians who drank tea seemed to dunk a teabag in hot water as I had found to my cost when Mario's mother had offered to make me some in Naples that weekend. I had watched in disbelief as she heated some water to blood temperature in a saucepan before throwing in a Lipton's tea bag and pouring the contents into a large cup. On the surface were gobbets of what looked like olive oil, presumably from the pan, which was clearly more often used to make some of Consiglia's delicious pasta sauces than it was for making tea.

"Looks as if I'll have to do without my morning cup of tea then. And my toast for that matter." I had yet to see an electric toaster in Italy, and this shop in Terni was no exception.

"Don't worry. I'll make you tea every morning and bring it to you in bed." After spending so much time in my company Mario actually made a very passable cup of tea these days. He had even started drinking it himself in the morning, instead of the coffee that he had been brought up on at home.

"But I hope you're not going to expect me to eat that revolting brown stuff you spread on your toast."

It took me a while to work out that he meant my Marmite, brought in at the bottom of my suitcase every time I went to England.

"You must be joking. It's far too precious to waste on someone whose idea of a good breakfast is a few biscuits soaked in *caffelatte.*" I gave him a lingering kiss. "And while we're on the subject, when are you Italians going to learn how to make butter? The stuff you can buy here tastes more like cheese and it's totally the wrong colour."

Mario left earlier than usual that Sunday afternoon, as he said he needed time to pack all the things he would be taking to Rome for the big move in a few days' time. He also wanted to spend some time with his mother.

"It's going to be hard on her, not having me around anymore."

"But you're twenty six!"

"That's not the point. Italian families are very close and no one moves away from home till they have to. You hard-hearted English people will never be able to understand something like that."

I knew he was joking, but it riled me slightly nonetheless.

"Yes. Well some of us didn't have much choice," I replied.

I too had plenty to do before leaving for Rome to move into the flat the following Wednesday. I had to pack some smarter clothes in which to go to work each day and look presentable. It had been easy to get into the habit of wearing shorts or jeans here in San Massano, but I had noticed that the women all looked extremely chic in Rome. Even in the newsroom, people tended to be better dressed than the journalists back home. I had booked an appointment at a hairdresser I had found in Lavena and I needed to get in some supplies to cook dinner for Angela and Ercolino the following evening. Ercolino seemed to have accepted my decision, but he still looked wounded every time I saw him and I felt an inexplicable sense of guilt, so I had invited them both round on Tuesday evening. I also had to phone my brothers in England. It had been several weeks since we last spoke, and although they knew about Mario, they had no idea I

179

was about to move in with him. I had a feeling that neither of them would be particularly thrilled by the news.

My Fiat 500 started first time when I set off next morning to Lavena. Thankfully, Mario had offered to come and pick me up on Wednesday morning to help me with my bags. I would never have been able to fit everything into my small car, and I was still wary of driving it to Rome. But here in the hills, the little yellow car was perfect and swung easily round the curves towards Lavena, with the soaring spectacle of the waterfalls in the far distance. I switched off the engine and shifted into neutral to coast down the last slope into the pretty hill town. Out of the corner of my eye, I glimpsed the pink hoarding outside the newspaper shop.

"Pensioner killed by bees."

The traffic policeman was in his usual place and waved a friendly greeting, before fishing out his whistle and directing me into a small space right outside his sisters' shop. He moved towards me and bent down to open the door, as he always did.

"*Buongiorno Signorina*. Allow me. You should try the melons that have just arrived. They are quite exceptional." He blew his whistle again and poked his head through the multi-coloured plastic fronds that hung from the open door of his sisters' shop in a vain bid to keep the flies out.

"Anna. Margherita! The *signorina inglese* is here to do her shopping. She hasn't got all day, so stop gossiping and get on and serve her."

I had become used to receiving this kind of service since I started shopping regularly at the Lavena store. I occasionally felt a twinge about not giving the village shop in San Massano more business, but the choice there was so very limited and things had become even worse in the last few weeks. On the few occasions I had walked up to the piazza to buy a last minute tin of tomatoes Tito had been standing behind the counter, gazing listlessly at the almost empty shelves. On the wall behind him, Clara smiled down from a poster-sized framed photograph taken on her wedding day to Tito. The old man had lost weight, so that his clothes hung loosely on his already thin frame, and the few wisps of white hair that stuck out unevenly on the sides and back of his head were in urgent need of a trim.

"Oh. It's you *Signorina*. I didn't hear you come in. I'm afraid I'm not quite myself at the moment. To tell the truth, I don't think I ever will be. You can't imagine how lonely it is for me now. I miss her every single second of the day and night." He wiped away a tear with a handkerchief from the breast pocket of his uncharacteristically grimy white coat, which had one sleeve inexpertly sewn with a wide black hoop. The shopkeeper's eyes had glazed over by now and he stared vacantly down at his hands, playing with the two gold bands on his thin ring finger, his shoulders hunched in grief. With a sudden shudder, he appeared to collect his thoughts and pulled himself up straight again.

"I'm sorry *Signorina*. Please forgive me. Was there something that you wanted?"

Tito and his sad decline was still on my mind when I drove back up the winding lanes to San Massano several hours later, my hair freshly cut and several plastic bags on the back seat of the car packed with wine, pasta, fresh tomatoes, mozzarella, several thick sprigs of basil and, gently perched on top of the other groceries, some of the season's first green figs. The sisters told me they had been freshly picked from their own tree that morning and split one in half to let me try the dark red flesh, pitted with tiny pale seeds. Margherita, the younger of the two shopkeepers, sliced off a sliver of their local cured prosciutto from a huge joint impaled on a wrought iron clamp.

"This is the way to eat figs," she said, handing me a small piece of fig and prosciutto between her thumb and forefinger.

She was right. It was delicious and would be perfect for the *antipasto* when Angela and Ercolino came to dinner the following evening. I ordered some prosciutto to go with them. Margherita divided the rest of the fig and prosciutto into two small portions and handed one to her sister. With what looked like a carefully synchronised movement, the two women raised their elbows and popped the morsels into their open mouths.

Something was different, but with thoughts of Tito still in my mind as I passed the layby a few hundred yards out of Lavena I couldn't quite put my finger on what it was. This was the place where the camper van was usually parked, with its owner engrossed in crossword puzzles as she waited for her next client to draw up in his car and knock on the side door. Today, there was no camper van, and no sign of the woman either. In their usual place was a tatty old stuffed chair, its blue fabric faded by age and the sun. A dark-skinned girl with long black hair was seated on it, her legs crossed provocatively beneath an extremely short mini skirt made of shiny red plastic. She pouted seductively as she saw my car pass, raising a hand and half rising out of her chair to stop me. Her expression turned to one of disappointment when she saw who was driving and she sat back down on her seat to wait for a better opportunity.

At first it was the seemingly inconsequential details of daily life that proved most difficult. Mario, who had watched his mother make *gnocchi* since he was a small boy, believed that the best way to boil potatoes was with the skin on, then to peel them once they were cooked.

"That stops all the water getting into the flesh of the potato and making them mushy," he told me, looking over my shoulder with a critical eye. I was busy peeling potatoes with a blunt kitchen knife, in the absence of a potato peeler. Mashing them proved to be another bone of contention. I had brought my old potato masher with me from San Massano, which in turn had come over with me on one of my trips from England. I had never seen one for sale here in Italy.

"What a very strange system. It looks like an awful lot of hard work, and look, it's still lumpy."

After five minutes' solid mashing, I had to admit privately – though certainly not to Mario – that the results were not as smooth as I had hoped. And mashing potatoes in the heat of a warm and humid kitchen in Rome was very different from doing the same procedure on a chilly evening back home.

I was not attempting to make *gnocchi*. I had decided that on this our first evening together in our new flat that I should cook something quintessentially English. I had spent the past hour and a half in the kitchen making a chicken and leek pie, with home-made pastry, to be served with the less than perfect mashed potatoes and carrots, boiled in a little water with sugar and butter. Mario eyed them doubtfully.

"You have to eat everything together I suppose?"

I explained the idea of trying to put a small piece of everything on the same fork.

"That way, all the flavours blend together."

He didn't look very convinced.

"And what are these green things inside the pie?"

I had spent some time trawling the local market that morning to track down a source of leeks, and had felt triumphant when I had at last spotted a few stringy specimens on a stall presided over by a frail-looking old lady with two chipped front teeth. Leeks were not vegetables that featured very strongly in the daily lives of most Italians, it seemed.

Later, as we sat over the half empty plates and dishes, the telephone rang from the living room. Mario got up to answer it and I sat twirling the glass of red wine in my hand, putting off the moment when it would be time to start washing the plates and pans. I reflected, not for the first time that evening, on how strange it was not having any of the gadgets and appliances that I had taken for granted in my other life. Here, there was no dishwasher, and not even a washing machine. And while in San Massano, washing my clothes and bed linen out in the bathtub once a week seemed part of the whole adventure, here in Rome I wasn't quite so sure.

The phone call seemed to go on forever. Through the half-open door into the living room came snatches of conversation, about the flat, Mario's first day in his new job and other details of his day so far. It must be his mother.

"Then there's a sort of covering on the top which goes hard when you put it in the oven."

There was a long pause before he spoke again.

"Well it was a bit dry," I heard him reply.

It was ages since I had ironed a shirt. The last time I had done it was when my mother had been ill in hospital and she had asked me to make sure that my father had something clean to wear for work. With the help of the shiny steam iron that was kept in the laundry, next to the washing machine and tumble dryer, I had soon got the hang of it, though I couldn't say I particularly enjoyed it. In all the three years we had lived together in Brighton, I had never ironed a single shirt for Rob. I wasn't planning to do it for Mario either, but watching him struggle with the ancient looking iron that the doctor's wife had left for us, I grabbed it from his hand. There was no ironing board, so the only way to do it was to lay a towel flat on the table. I spread his white shirt out on top and pressed the iron to the collar. There was a faint whiff of singeing.

"Um. I'm sorry, the iron must have had something stuck to it." It was his best shirt, one that he had bought the day before from a smart men's outfitters a few streets away from our flat.

"I'll buy you another one tomorrow," I said lamely.

I soon had almost more work than I could handle. As well as my shifts in Via Ripetta and the articles I wrote for newspapers in England, the US, Australia and Canada, I had recently been taken on as the Italy correspondent of the Washington Post. The news editor was abrasive and charmless and thought nothing of ringing me at two in the morning, when it was still the afternoon where he was. But the connection proved a useful one in many other ways and I soon found I had no trouble in getting interviews with just about anyone I needed to talk to and I found myself being invited to a constant stream of press conferences and receptions. Before long, another job landed in my lap. This one was an agency run by a dynamic Frenchwoman called Christine who had lived for many years in the US and had found backers to set up a news business. The agency would supply news to newspapers in North Africa, the Middle East and Asia, she told me when we met for a coffee at a stylish bar in Piazza Navona. She was looking for someone with a good news background to write some articles out of Italy and then maybe to do some travelling. It sounded too good to be true.

It was mid-November and the trees in the park next to our flat had turned a spectacular shade of rich yellow. Each one had a circle of fallen leaves on the grass around its trunk. Mario and I were sitting at the circular glass-topped table on our terrace, drinking a glass of wine before dinner. Unlike San Massano, where the winter was already settling in, the weather was still mild here in Rome and we were both wearing light sweaters.

It was now almost three months since we had moved in together and although the feeling of mutual attraction was still very strong, there was an undercurrent of tension in our relationship that both of us tried to ignore. It was obvious that Mario found it hard being away from his huge family. Neither of us really knew anyone in Rome, except for the contacts we made through work. And I had to admit that I found it difficult living with someone who had been used to having all his meals cooked for him and his clothes laundered for him by his mother and sister – not that he had asked me to do any more ironing after my first disastrous attempt. Mario clearly found my slovenly ways frustrating and I had come back from the newspaper one day to find the top of the cooker neatly lined with silver foil. It looked horrible.

"What on earth is that for?" It had been a stressful day and I still had to talk to my news editor in Washington about a piece he wanted on the mafia.

"It's so that we don't always have a filthy stove. Seeing that you don't seem to like cleaning it, we can just change the silver paper when it gets dirty."

My expression must have made it clear that I was totally mystified.

"Look, the way I was brought up, you clean the cooker and all the kitchen surfaces every time you cook a meal. Then you wash the floor and open the windows to let in some fresh air." He pointed to a mop and bucket in the corner of the kitchen. I looked at it blankly.

"Why on earth would you want to do that?"

A visit from Mario's mother a couple of weeks earlier did little to help the situation. Determined to make a success of the occasion, I had tidied up the flat as best I could and bought some flowers from the market to place on the small table next to the sofa bed where she would be sleeping in the living room. The flat was barely big enough for two people and there was no spare bedroom. The living room doubled up as my study, with a desk squeezed into one corner.

At first, things had gone well and there had been a sense of festivity bordering on euphoria as mother and son were reunited in a tight embrace. Emerging from the lift outside our front door, Consiglia clutched a large dark red plastic holdall. She laid it on the table and unzipped it to reveal several small packages, each one wrapped in different coloured paper. Inside one was a length of Neapolitan salame, its peppery red flesh sweating as she drew it out of its wrapper. Another contained a triangular slab of pale coloured cheese.

"*Provolone!*"

Consiglia had also brought a contraption that looked like a giant garlic crusher, which Mario told me was what Italians used to mash potatoes. He must have asked her to bring it to save him from more evenings of my lumpy mashed potato. From the bottom of the holdall, his mother drew out an aluminium container wrapped in foil and swathed in several layers of cling film. Unwrapping it carefully to avoid spilling the red-coloured oil that was trapped under the packaging, she revealed a huge dish of *parmigiana di melanzane*. She held it out to me.

"I remember how much you loved it when you came to my house, so I made this especially for you." And she wrapped me in a warm hug, the smell of her rich perfume mingling with the unmistakable whiff of garlic and olive oil.

I had seen photographs of Consiglia when she was a striking 25-year-old, her dark shoulder-length hair swept back by a light breeze and her wide generous mouth smiling into the camera to reveal well-shaped white teeth. They reminded me of Mario's. She was still a good-looking woman, and for this visit she had gone to considerable trouble to look her best. She was wearing a beige silk blouse and a well-tailored cream and brown skirt, with a pair of elegant heeled tan-coloured leather shoes to match. On her wrist was an assortment of gold bangles and some small ruby earrings sparkled from beneath her hair, which had been freshly styled and coloured.

My good intentions received their first setback barely an hour into the visit, when a terrible transformation took place. Off came the silk blouse and on went a shapeless cotton shift and some pale green flip-floppy slippers. It wasn't long before our guest was rushing around the flat, tidying up the piles of newspapers and cuttings which were strewn on almost every available surface. She tore open the fridge and proceeded to cook most of the contents, chopping, grating, frying and simmering in a non-stop frenzy. The freezer's meagre contents were removed, scanned for sell-by-dates and discarded or left to defrost, to be turned into more dishes at the earliest possible opportunity. Meanwhile, she grabbed a broom to begin a bout of relentless sweeping, poking the brush under my desk and between my feet as I sat at my desk trying to write an article about an eruption of Mount Etna for the next morning's edition of the Washington Post.

The following day, after Mario had left for work, things began to deteriorate even further. It started with Consiglia dusting my desk as I was doing a phone interview with a drug squad official who was giving me figures about an important cocaine haul at Fiumicino airport. I settled down to write the article, trying to ignore the clattering of pots and pans now coming from the kitchen and making it impossible to concentrate. Unable to contain my frustration any longer, I called out and begged for her to be a little quieter. Contrite, she now began tiptoeing around, sweeping very slowly and opening and closing doors and cupboards with great care and exaggerated precision, which was of course just as distracting. The lowest ebb in our relationship came the next morning, when Consiglia insisted on stripping our bed in some form of archaic post-nuptial rite. I blew a fuse, though I regretted it immediately and felt dreadful for the rest of her stay.

A few days later, with Mario's mother gone and tempers more or less restored, we settled back into our old routine. Late on a Friday afternoon, come what may, we always packed a weekend bag with a few clothes and a large wicker basket with some food and wine and settled into Mario's car for the drive to San Massano. My nerves were already less stretched at the prospect of two days in the house that I thought of as home, where there would be no deadlines and nothing more pressing than the need to collect some kindling wood and build a fire in the big old hearth that dominated the sitting room. I could feel the tensions in my jaw muscles melt away as we rounded the final curve and the lovely old stone built house loomed into view.

The following morning we could stay in bed as long as we liked and I would run a long hot bath and make two mugs of scalding tea before we both gingerly lowered ourselves in the boiling water and watched our limbs turn pink. It was the most effective way of getting warm in a house that still had no heating except for the open fire.

"It's much too hot!" Mario would invariably say with a sharp intake of breath seconds after putting in his big toe to test the water.

"It's just the first few seconds. Come on." We could hardly see each other across the steam that rose in billows as hot water met ice cold air, but I would take him by the hand and gently draw him down into the bathtub facing me, and there we would stay, legs entwined, the water up to our necks, sipping tea and making plans for the rest of the weekend that lay before us.

At times like that, I thought nothing could spoil our happiness. Removed from the outside world, I felt totally content to spend long hours doing very little in the company of the man I loved, and I know Mario felt just the same. There was a lazy pattern to our days. What was left of the morning would be spent gathering and stacking firewood or going for a stroll up the ancient mule path that left from the property and trailed along the crest of the hill and back down into the village. Then we would plan a long lunch, based on bruschetta grilled over the fire and pasta cooked by Mario. The wine was almost always a rich ruby red local *San*

Giovese from nearby Amelia, which we bought in 5-litre flagons from the sisters' grocery store in Lavena. Served in my parents' fine crystal glasses, the food set out on hand-painted red and white ceramic dishes that Mario had bought me for my birthday, the meal was eaten at a table in front of the log fire. Later, when the plates were empty and the glasses had been refilled, we would drag the table to one side and pull the leather sofa up to take its place, before stretching out together, my head on Mario's chest, talking and dozing until the cold air alerted us to the fact that the fire had finally gone out.

That year proved to be one of the coldest on record. Day after day, the merciless *tramontana* wind blew in from the north, bringing with it a bitter chill that crept in to your bones. Even the hardy villagers of San Massano, who were used to braving freezing temperatures with nothing to protect them but an extra sweater and a thicker pair of coarse woollen socks, started to spend more time in front of their log fires, only venturing out in the mornings and early evenings to feed their animals and inspect their ailing olive trees. There wasn't a single family in the village that didn't have at least fifty trees on its land, and these were an important source of income as well as the oil they yielded for household use. Now, in swathes across the hills from Lavena to San Massano, scores and scores of the delicate silvery trees were dying, unable to withstand the biting cold that had frozen their roots solid in the ground and had withered the leaves on their branches. The same was happening across the rest of central Italy as winter tightened its grip yet further. The olive oil industry was facing ruin, and with it thousands of small-scale farmers who depended on it for their living. Questions were asked in parliament and representations made to the European Union. At last came some good news. A subsidy would be made available of 10,000 lire for every tree that had been lost.

The night of January 27 that year was one that no one would forget for a very long time. I knew I certainly wouldn't. The day had started with more blustery winds. It was a Saturday, and the *giorno della merla* – the coldest day of the whole year in Italy, according to tradition. The shutters banged outside our bedroom window and a whistling sound echoed through the house. I snuggled close to Mario under the weight of the extra blankets we had piled on before going to bed. On the window a few feet away from where we lay, crystals of ice sparkled on both sides of the glass pane. The cost of replacing the ancient wooden window frames had been too high when Cesare had drawn up the estimate for the renovation, but I was now beginning to regret not having somehow found the money. The thought of leaving the warmth of the bed to brave the icy cold temperature of the rest of the house was very unappealing. Even the prospect of a hot bath was not enough to draw me out. I knew that sliding into the scalding water would be even more excruciating on a bitterly cold day like today. We burrowed further down still under the covers, daring each other to find the courage to get up and discussing what we could take that evening to Angela and Ercolino's place. They had invited us up to their house in the village for dinner.

The jolt that shook us from our torpor was quite unlike anything I had ever felt before. It seemed to grab hold of the old iron bedstead and shake it uncontrollably. From the other rooms came sounds of crashing plates and glasses.

"An earthquake! Quick. Under the bed." Mario leapt, pulling me after him and we lay shivering on the cold stone floor.

He had been a teenager when the big earthquake had hit Avellino outside Naples during the winter of 1981 and he had often described to me the terror of that night, which had left thousands of people dead in the rubble and many more without

191

a home. I had felt a few small tremors since coming to San Massano, hearing the crockery rattle on the shelves and seeing a dandruff-like patina of dust settle over the furniture. But although these shocks were unnerving, they were over soon enough and, to be honest, they gave me more of a secret thrill than any sense of real fear.

This one was very different and I instinctively knew it was serious. The trembling seemed to go on for an incalculably long time, though it turned out it was actually just over a minute and a half when the newspapers reported on it next day. Even so, that was well over twice as long as the average tremor in this part of the Appenines and its magnitude was one of the highest for many years.

Miraculously, no one had been killed, but the damage was considerable. Half an hour later, up in San Massano, there was a sombre mood as villagers surveyed the scene. Several houses had lost part of the roof. Small piles of masonry were scattered here and there along the narrow streets. Tito wandered around forlornly. His house had been saved, but the quake had sent the photograph of Clara crashing to the floor, where it lay now, the glass shattered into a hundred tiny pieces.

"You look a bit miserable. What on earth's the matter? And what have you done with Mario?" Angela held her arms out to me and gave me an affectionate hug. Another two months had passed and I was on my own for the first time since Mario and I had moved in together. He had chosen not to come to San Massano with me this weekend, saying that he wanted to go down to Naples to visit his family and see some of his friends. He had invited me to go with him, but hadn't pressed me when I had hesitated. If I was really honest, I was quite relieved at the prospect of having some time to myself. I needed to think, and to try and understand what was happening between us. Both of us knew that something was very wrong, although neither had brought the subject out into the open. There had been a few arguments, followed by a brooding silence that sometimes lasted for days on end, and although we still shared a flat, we were spending less and less time in each other's company. We seemed to be drifting apart.

"Mario hasn't come up this weekend. Actually, I think it might be over."

"But why? You looked so happy together the last time I saw you. Here, have a glass of wine and tell me all about it."

Angela was the most understanding person I had ever met and it wasn't until I was sitting at her kitchen table a few minutes later that I realised how much I had needed to talk to someone. Ercolino was down in Terni taking Mamma to the chiropodist, so there would be no interruptions. She handed me a half-filled tumbler of white wine and poured one for herself.

"I can't really explain it. He hasn't done anything wrong as such, and I'm very very fond of him. But I sometimes wonder where it's all heading. All my friends back home have got high-powered careers and are settling down to get married, and we just drift along from day to day without making any plans. He doesn't seem to have any sense of urgency at all."

We were on to our second glass of wine now. Angela lit a cigarette, and let me carry on talking.

"Then there are all the differences between our cultures. It makes every little thing more difficult, every single thing. And no one really thinks our relationship is a good idea. Not his family – although they are very nice to me – nor mine, or at least what's left of it. Even Ercolino thinks I'm making a big mistake."

"Don't take any notice of Ercolino. He's a fine one to talk." Angela refilled our glasses. "People who are close to you both just want to protect you, but at the end of the day it's you who has to make the decision, and then bear the consequences if it doesn't work out."

She lit another cigarette and took a long sip from her glass.

"After all these years, my own father still hasn't spoken to me because I married Ercolino, and that has been extremely hard for me," she said. "I have no regrets because I love Ercolino very much and I know he adores me too. In a way I've been lucky, but it's also been very lonely. I suppose what I'm saying is that if you're really sure that you have found the right person, then don't let anyone stand in your way. But as our marriage shows, it's not all plain sailing, and there are a great many sacrifices you will have to make. So just be very certain before you do anything that you might come to regret."

Although there was no proof, I strongly suspected that Mario had had more or less the same conversation that weekend down in Naples, perhaps with a friend or, more likely, with his closest cousin Lorenzo. Whatever the truth, by the time he came back on Sunday evening there seemed to be an unspoken understanding between us that it was time to go our separate ways. Although we still ate together in the evenings and shared the same bed at night, the silences between us became longer and deeper until, a few days later, fate finally took a hand. In a telephone call, Christine, the head of the news agency I had now been working for since January, asked me to have lunch with her the following day. She had something important that she wanted to discuss. The agency was doing better than expected and the backers had agreed to open a small bureau in New York, she told me when we met at a quiet restaurant serving fish in a narrow street off the busy Campo de' Fiori in central Rome. She would be running the commercial side of the business, and she wondered if I would like to join her there to take care of the reporting.

Mario took the news with apparent equanimity, confirming, if there had been any need, that he had been planning his own exit strategy. He said he would move out by the end of the month, not to Naples, but to somewhere outside Rome, so he could keep his job. He couldn't ask to be transferred back again now, and in any case, he didn't feel like moving back to Naples. I would stay on at the flat for another month, to see out the contract and organise all the things that would have to be sorted before I left on June 1st. I felt my heart wrench as I thought about closing up the house at San Massano.

My thoughts were interrupted by the sound of the telephone ringing in the living room. Mario got up to answer it, looking relieved to have the chance to escape the maudlin conversation.

"It's for you," he called from next door. "It's Ercolino. He says he has something to tell you."

I took the receiver from him and held it to my ear.

"Listen, I've got some very sad news to tell you, but I thought you ought to know, seeing that you're one of the village now."

"What is it Ercolino? What's happened?"

"It's Tito. It all got too much for him. He's as dead as a doormat. One of his sisters has found him hanged in the back of the shop."

Chapter Ten

The shiny walnut coffin wound its way up the narrow alleyways of San Massano, shouldered by Agostino, Fabrizio and four other young men who, judging by their same close set eyes and long thin noses were Tito's nephews from Terni. Leading the procession was Don Gaetano, flanked by two altar boys, who waved canisters of incense in time with each rhythmic step of the procession. Although Tito had taken his own life, the priest had agreed to give him a Christian funeral. Don Gaetano had no great liking for the people of this wayward village, but he had yielded to the pleas of the dead man's two sisters, both respectable women who went to Mass every Sunday with their husbands. The third sister, who lived in Australia, had not had time to make the journey, but had sent a wreath of gladioli and palm leaves, with a black edged card bearing the message: To my dear brother. May God forgive you.

Afterwards, outside the tiny church, where Tito and Clara had been married less than a year earlier, the mourners gathered in the late spring sunshine. Part of the church's terracotta roof had been damaged by the earthquake, and half of the building was still swathed in scaffolding, though the workmen had respectfully withdrawn for the duration of the service. There were no tears – the shopkeeper had been nearly sixty when he died – but a pall of grim resignation hung over the group. All of them had lived through hard times, some more than others, and few had any illusions about what lay ahead.

"What can you do?" muttered one of the village women helplessly. Another shrugged her shoulders.

"It's just the way it is."

Word had already got round that I would soon be leaving San Massano, and somehow the entire village seemed to know why.

"I hear you've broken up with your young man," said Settima in a matter-of-fact way. We were waiting for the funeral procession to start its descent on the final journey to the cemetery. "Never mind. There's plenty more fish in the sea."

Generosa also had some practical advice to offer.

"I'll be sad to see you go *Stella*," she said and clutched me to her enormous chest. "But seeing as how you're leaving, why don't I put in a claim for all those olive trees on your land? They're worth 10,000 lire each, you know. If you drop round and sign the forms before you go, I'll take care of all the rest and it will be no problem saying that they were all lost in the frost. Then we can split the difference."

It was hard not to smile at Generosa's roguery. It seemed a long time since I had smiled at all.

"You're looking very thin. Is it the business with the boyfriend from Naples?" Elisa who owned the bar in Montebello stepped forward and kissed me on both cheeks.

"It's not worth making yourself unhappy over a man. What's he done? Run off with some other woman, I suppose. Well don't let it get to you."

Elisa was right about one thing. I had lost a great deal of weight in the last few unhappy weeks and when I looked in the mirror, I could see my cheeks looked sunken and my skin was sallow.

There were still several weeks before I was due to leave Italy and move to New York, but it felt as if the farewells had already started. At every turn, there were arrangements to be made and goodbyes to be said. Benedetto came up to look at some of the work that still needed doing. I had no intention of selling my lovely house, but who knows how often I would be able to get back to see it and I certainly didn't want to leave it in a state of disrepair. Accompanied as always by Caterina perched next to him in his *Ape*, the village odd job man made a mental note of some of the various tasks that would have to be taken care of, inside the house and outside in the garden. I still hadn't got round to tiling the bathroom, but that was too much of a specialised job for Benedetto and he said he would send up someone who would be able to do it. Having these conversations was reminiscent of the first few months after I had bought the house, but it was certainly a great deal less fun this time around.

I had decided to leave my Fiat 500 at the house when I left, rather than taking it down to dirty Paolo's garage. If I opened the doors under the main arch and revved the car sharply to get it up the grass slope, I could just about squeeze it in with a couple of inches to spare on either side. Agostino had shown me how to remove the battery so that it wouldn't corrode and I now did a practice run to make sure there would be no last minute problems. I would miss my little yellow car and stroked it affectionately before pulling on the handbrake and stepping out.

Mario had moved out by the time I arrived back at the Rome flat later that weekend. On his side of the wardrobe, there was an empty space where his clothes had once hung. He had taken some crockery and tumblers for the tiny bedsit he had rented on the outskirts of the city. There was a note on the table, pinned down by a ceramic vase he had once given me.

"*Sorry to have taken the coward's way out but I thought it best for both of us to avoid a last goodbye. Hope you don't mind me taking a few plates and glasses for my little hovel.*"

I didn't mind at all. I certainly wouldn't be needing them. I had never felt less like eating in my life.

Tossing and turning in the big heavy bed that first night on my own, I had plenty of time to think about what had gone wrong between Mario and I, but I was no nearer to reaching an understanding. Now that he was gone I missed him more than I could say. I wondered what his new flat was like and what he was doing. I hoped he was alone and buried my head in the pillow, trying not to imagine those warm green eyes locked into another woman's gaze.

"You look as if you've lost a shilling and picked up three pennies."

"It's sixpence."

"What?"

"It's sixpence, not three pennies."

"Oh. What a bloody stupid language. Anyway, you look about as miserable as I feel. You may be a pain in the neck but Angela and I are both going to miss you very much."

The moment I had been dreading had finally come. My bags were packed and ready by the front door, the fridge had been emptied and unplugged and the house had been scrubbed and mopped. Mario would have been proud of me, I thought wryly. Ercolino had come to take me to the station in Terni, where I would catch the train to Rome. I had one last night in the flat before my flight left for New York the following day. Angela had come up to the house with Ercolino, but after a few minutes she had said she was going outside to smoke a cigarette and would wait for us in the car down below.

"She's taken it rather badly you know." He took hold of one of my suitcases. "And so have I come to that. We thought we meant more to you than this. I don't understand why you have to go away, just because you've split up with your boyfriend."

"I'm going to work in New York," I said softly. "It's what I've always wanted."

199

"It doesn't look as if you're so bloody thrilled about it. You certainly could have fooled me."

There was a painful silence in the car during the twenty minute journey to Terni. Even Ercolino, who was rarely lost for words, could find little to say beyond occasional muttered expressions of disbelief, punctuated by an exaggerated shrugging of shoulders, a gesture that I knew meant that someone had done something unbelievably stupid. From the back, where Angela was crammed in uncomfortably with my luggage, came a series of stifled sighs. Ercolino turned on the radio, and a plaintive ballad blared out of the tiny speakers.

Non mi lasciare. Sarai nel mio cuore per sempre!

I had been fighting a losing battle to stay on top of the tears that had been welling up in me since early that morning, and the mellifluous lyrics, accompanied by a haunting melody that had been playing on every radio station in those first few weeks with Mario, sent my reserve crashing. Ercolino turned off the radio abruptly.

"I thought you were glad to be leaving us?"

"Don't start shouting. You'll only make it worse." Angela's gentle voice came from the rear of the car and she placed a hand on mine.

"You will write to me, won't you? You won't just disappear?"

There was no friendly family to share their picnic with me on this last train journey to Rome. I unwrapped the package that Angela had pressed into my hand a few minutes before the train pulled out of Terni station. There was a sandwich, made from two slabs of white bread filled with slices of pecorino cheese and prosciutto and a small box of red wine with a plastic straw, like a children's juice carton. I jabbed the straw into the box and took a long pull on the warm red wine. This time tomorrow I'd be on the plane to New York, ready to start my new life. I took a bite of the sandwich, and tried in vain to swallow it. I took another swig from the wine box to wash it down. Then, ignoring the puzzled gaze of the middle-aged couple sitting opposite, I stood up, drew down the window and hurled the sandwich out, watching it disappear as the olive trees and fields full of yellow broom hurtled by.

For someone who hated cleaning as much as I did, it was ironic that I was spending my last twenty four hours in Italy doing just that. The doctor's wife had left me in no doubt whatsoever that the flat in Rome would need to be spotless if I wanted to get back the 200,000 lire deposit that Mario and I had paid when we had taken on the lease. So with only an afternoon and evening to get everything done, as well as all the packing for my departure the following morning, I reluctantly took hold of a broom from the kitchen cupboard and set to work to sweep the dusty floors. Somewhere in the back of my mind was a vague realisation that I was doing things the wrong way round. Weren't you supposed to dust the furniture and wipe the surfaces before you cleaned the floor?

"Too bad," I muttered to myself, putting down the broom and reaching for the bucket and mop. If there was one thing that I certainly wouldn't miss it would be cleaning floors with a mop. Hadn't anyone heard of a vacuum cleaner? I wondered idly what my apartment would be like in New York. The news agency had rented one for me, and I had been told that it was small, though in a very good location on the Upper West Side, just off Central Park. It would be exciting to live in Manhattan. Mario and I had often talked about taking a trip there and whiling away the evenings in sleazy jazz bars, just as we'd seen in a film that we'd watched one evening at the flat here in Rome. My glance fell on the overstuffed sofa where we had been sitting that evening, just a few feet away, his arm around my shoulders, my head resting on his chest, his other hand lightly touching my leg, tracing the seams of my jeans with his fingers.

"We'll go to the best jazz club in town," he had said, leaning towards me to kiss me on the lips. "And then we'll get a yellow cab home to bed." He had kissed me again, longer this time. "And in the morning, I'll bring you bagels for your breakfast."

I had been doing quite well up until then, the pressure of all that needed doing deliberately pushing all other thoughts from my mind. But now, as I looked at the sofa where Mario and I had sat so contentedly that evening, the barriers came crashing down again and for the third time that day I found myself sobbing. I leaned on the mop and stared miserably out of the window at the tops of the plane trees that lined the busy avenue. From down below came the sound of Rome's relentless traffic and mothers shouting at their children, trying to make their voices heard above the din.

It would be hard to say how long I stayed like that, staring blankly through the glass without bothering to wipe the tears that were streaming down my face. Somewhere deep in the back of my mind was a nagging voice telling me that I still had so much to do, and that I must get on. But somehow the words didn't get through. I stood there aimlessly, the front of my tee-shirt now quite sodden.

I never heard the sound of the key in the lock. And I didn't notice the footsteps as they crept up behind me. But when I smelt that familiar mixture of soap and aftershave and felt a warm grip on my shoulder, something slowly began to register. Another hand now reached out gently in front of me. I looked at it stupidly, unable to take it in. It was holding a small bunch of freesias, tied with a pale green bow. Nestling in the centre was a small box, propped open to reveal something sparkling. I turned round, unable to take it in, and saw a pair of green eyes gazing intently into mine.

"So will you?" It was Mario who spoke first.

"Will I what?" My voice had an unpleasant nasal twang, I noticed, the result of so much crying.

"Marry me, of course. That's why I've come back."

I said yes, though even as the words left my mouth my head was spinning with all that it would mean. Where would we live now that we were giving up the flat? What about my job? And more immediately, what about New York, where I was due to be heading to start a new life in approximately twelve hours? Mario had already thought about all these problems, which he assured me were minor hurdles. Pouring me a glass of champagne from a bottle that he had brought with him, he settled me down on the sofa to explain his ideas.

"First of all, I will talk to the doctor's wife and ask her to extend our lease for another couple of months while we look for a new apartment. Unless you want to stay on here of course?"

I shook my head. The place had taken on so many unhappy memories, and if I was honest, I had never much liked living in what felt like someone else's flat with all their furniture and their paintings on the walls.

"As for New York, I suggest you call the agency and explain what has happened and just see what they say. Here, give me the number and I'll dial it for you."

It was comforting to have Mario's calm presence next to me once again and to talk things through with him and make plans for the future.

"I do love you very much," I told him, pulling him back on to the sofa as he moved towards the phone to make the call. He kissed me softly and dabbed my mascara streaked cheeks with a handkerchief.

"So do I. More than I can say. It's been miserable these past few weeks living without you. I don't want us ever to be parted again."

In fact, we were parted the very next morning. After the initial shock of hearing my news, Christine had suggested that I come to New York as planned, but just for a month. I could help her to get the news side of the business up and running and meanwhile she would do everything possible to think of a solution that would enable me to work for the agency from Italy. It was too good an opportunity to miss, though it was wretched having to say goodbye so soon after having found each other once again. Mario drove me to the airport, only taking his hand off my knee to change gear.

"It's just for a short time, then we'll be together for always." Mario hugged me in a tight embrace and kissed me on the lips. We were at the departure gate now and I was crying again.

"Go on. Off you go, or your mascara will run again." One last kiss. "And don't go to too many jazz bars."

During the next few weeks, we spoke by phone as often as we could afford it, which was once every two or three days. The rest of the time we communicated by fax, writing each other long love letters, each sighing late into the night as we read and reread them. Thinking of Mario made it hard to appreciate the wonder of Manhattan, and I longed for him to be with me as I walked through Central Park, past the John Lennon memorial each day on my way to work, with the New York skyline etched out dramatically in the early morning sun. As for the sleazy jazz bars, they would have to wait until we could both come back to New York together. Christine had already worked out that the agency would open a European bureau, which I could run out of Rome. If the business took off, and it looked as if it might, there would be plenty of opportunities to come back to New York in the future.

Deciding where we would live also proved to be simpler than I had dared to hope. Mario had been to see the doctor's wife and she had agreed to extend the lease for a further two months.

That left us a month to find a new flat and to buy some furniture once I was back from New York.

"This time, we're not going to camp out amongst someone else's clutter," said Mario firmly. We were in his car on the way back from the airport. I touched the single red rose that he had given me as we clasped each other in the arrivals lounge, where he had been waiting for my flight to arrive.

"I couldn't agree more. I never want to sleep in anyone else's bed ever again. And this time, it would be nice to live somewhere a bit more central. Somewhere in the old part of Rome. Somewhere with a bit more soul."

The flat, when we found it, was just about perfect. It was half way up a sloping tree-lined avenue called Via Merulana, just a five-minute walk from the Colosseum. At either end of the road was a huge and splendid church – *Santa Maria Maggiore*, with a dramatic pyramid-shaped bell tower and soaring obelisk, and *San Giovanni in Laterano*, the world's most ancient church and the papal seat in Rome. A few yards up the hill from our apartment building was a small but pretty rose garden with an ancient Roman ruin, the auditorium of Mecenate, where Horace had read his poems to the leading intellectuals of the day more than two thousand years earlier.

"Does this have enough soul for you?" asked Mario.

"Buckets of it. I love it! It's just what I wanted."

The flat itself was in a gracious nineteenth century building, overlooking a quiet courtyard, with a small lodge manned by a porter and his wife. There were two high ceilinged bedrooms, a large living room with huge windows and a small kitchen and bathroom. For the moment it was entirely empty, with not even a kitchen cupboard or a light bulb. I was learning fast that unfurnished really meant just that here in Italy. Builders were painting the walls white and we were told that the place would be ready in two weeks. The whole flat had a light airy feel about it and I could not wait to move in.

"That gives us a fortnight to buy at least a bed, a kitchen table and some kitchen units. We can do the rest afterwards," said Mario. The woman from the rental agency drew out a contract from her briefcase and showed us where to sign.

We celebrated our find by having dinner at a small Sardinian *trattoria* tucked around the corner. The owner brought us the dish of the day – *ravioli* with a potato and mint filling – followed by spit-roast pork and wild artichokes, all served with *Vermentino* white wine. Afterwards there was pecorino cheese and a glass of *fil'e ferru*, the fiery Sardinian grappa.

"I think this should be our local." I felt heady with the wine, the grappa and the excitement of having found somewhere that would really be a home for both of us. "I just know we will be happy living here."

"It's going to be very, very complicated." The black-frocked priest, his thin lips puckering as he uttered his sombre verdict, pressed the tips of his fingers together and leaned across the table towards Mario and me.

"Are you sure you want to go ahead with this? I must warn you that you may well live to regret it. In my experience, mixed marriages rarely work." With thin greasy hair combed across a balding pate, his surplice straining to contain the bulk of his stomach, Monsignor Gabriele was an unprepossessing human being, and his words now, as we sat in his dark and gloomy office, filled me with dislike and resentment. We had driven up for the day to talk about plans for our wedding, which we wanted to be held in the *Abbazia di San Pietro in Valle*, a beautiful 7th century abbey nestling in the valley not far from Montebello. Monsignor Gabriele was in charge of all the church buildings in the diocese, and he appeared to be doing everything in his power to throw obstacles in our path. Not that he was alone in making life difficult. The Italian government was also doing its best to make the whole business as exasperating and stressful as it possibly could, and after enduring long queues at various council offices during the past few days we had been told we would need to present proof of payment of rubbish taxes and other vital scraps of paper culled from offices the length and breadth of Italy. Mario and I didn't fit into the usual mould, so we were to be punished with even more paperwork – he was Italian, I was British, he was born in Naples, we lived in Rome and were to be married in Umbria. The bureaucrats were having a field day.

For the Church, the difficulties were all too clear. My husband-to-be was Catholic, and I was Anglican. Monsignor Gabriele, who seemed incapable of smiling, sucked his teeth.

"If you do insist on going ahead with this, there is nothing I can do to stop you. But I must warn you that there is a fee for using our blessed abbey for weddings. The cost will be 300,000 lire, payable in cash."

The next stop was Naples, where we were summonsed to a meeting with the priest in charge of the diocese where Mario used to live. Church regulations stipulated that he would have to give his approval to our marriage. It was an open secret in the neighbourhood that this priest, Don Bernardo, had an illegitimate son. The boy was now in his teens and lived with his mother, who had been Don Bernardo's housekeeper. The priest ushered us into a dusty small room and told us to sit down on one of the hard-backed chairs that lined the wall. Overhead, a wooden statue of Christ on the cross, an abnormally large heart bursting grotesquely from his chest, looked down at our small party. As well as Mario and I, there was Consiglia, who had offered to come with us. The sun was still low in the sky, though it promised to be a stiflingly hot day, with not the slightest movement in the trees outside the window. Here in the priest's quarters, however, the atmosphere was distinctly frosty. There were no smiles from the austere-looking prelate, and certainly no good wishes for the future. The folds of his plump neck bulging over his dog collar, Don Bernardo looked us both up and down with a glacial expression.

"I understand that in clear contravention of the teachings of the Church, you have chosen to live together in sin before joining in holy matrimony. We take a very dim view of that, you know." He darted an accusing look in my direction.

"There is also the question of a Roman Catholic marrying a non-Catholic. That is something that the Church is not anxious to encourage. You young man." He pointed to Mario with a fat index finger. "Step into my office and let me ask you a few questions. I want to hear your answers to important issues, such as the sins of contraception, divorce and abortion. Only then can I make my decision." He turned towards me.

"After that, it will be your turn, so wait here until you are called. You may want to reflect in the meantime on the gravity of what you have done, and on what you are undertaking. Naturally, I shall be asking for a pledge that any children born from this, er, unorthodox union are educated in the holy Roman Catholic faith."

Returning to the uncomfortable chair to await my fire and brimstone inquisition, I was shaking with anger. My wise future mother-in-law whispered to me from the seat next to mine.

"Do you want to get married in church?"

"Yes, I do, very much, but this is intolerable."

"Then tell him whatever he wants to hear. Cross your fingers under the table. Do whatever it takes. But don't let him know what you really think. These priests are all the same."

Several hours later, seated at a wooden table outside a crowded *trattoria* just off one of the busiest squares in Naples, Mario was smiling.

"Well, I'm glad that's over. And at least he gave us the go ahead. I'd call that a definite victory." A waiter arrived and put down a carafe of red wine and a plate of deep-fried potato croquettes.

"They're the speciality of the house," said Consiglia, pushing the plate towards me across the paper tablecloth. "The old lady makes them. That's her, sitting in the corner." She pointed to a tiny bird-like woman sitting close by, her shoulders hunched over a tray of croquettes that she was preparing with badly arthritic fingers. Every so often, the old lady delved one hand into a pot of mashed potato, before stuffing a piece of mozzarella into the centre and rolling it out methodically on a flat board in front of her.

"A victory maybe, but at a price." I was still recovering from the encounter with the charmless priest. "You've got to do a course of ten lessons with the parish priest in Rome and I've got to find an Anglican priest to do the same for me. Then there's the small matter of the 100,000 lire that dear Don Bernardo asked for his consultation."

Consiglia laughed.

"Why do you think the Church is so wealthy? Anyway, Don Bernardo has to pay for his own past sins. I saw his boy the other day riding a brand new *motorino*."

My attention was distracted by the sight of a basket being lowered from the upstairs window of the *trattoria*. Down below, the waiter was involved in conversation with a young man who had drawn up to the pavement on his scooter. The young man handed over several packets of cigarettes, in exchange for a small wad of notes, before zooming off into the roar of the busy traffic. I watched fascinated as the waiter stuffed three packets into the basket and put one in his back pocket. He gave a sharp tug on the rope and a hand emerged from the window to haul the basket back up, together with its contents.

"They're contraband cigarettes, so they cost less," said Mario. "Everyone buys them around here."

"So what's with the basket and who were the cigarettes for?"

"Oh, that's just the quickest way of getting things without having to come all the way downstairs. Those cigarettes will be for clients who are eating inside – it's all part of the service. We Neapolitans are very inventive, especially when it comes to saving time and money."

The peace and stillness of San Massano after the noise and chaos of Naples was almost palpable. Mario and I had driven up to spend the weekend, after eating another plate of the old lady's potato croquettes and a pizza each, topped with cherry tomatoes, mozzarella and broad-leaved basil that tasted faintly of liquorice.

It was the first time we had been back to San Massano since I had left that sad day nearly five weeks earlier. The chattering of the house martins under the eaves broke the silence. There was my Fiat 500, just as I had left it. I ran my finger through the light layer of dust that had settled over the bright yellow paintwork. The keys to the house were where I had hidden them, hanging from an iron hook on a wooden beam in the *cantina*, beneath an old hand woven basket. My heart beating, I turned the largest of them in the lock of the heavy wooden door and pushed it open slowly. How wonderful it felt to be back.

"You took your bloody time. The pasta's almost ruined! Get a move on will you? I'm starvin' 'ungry."

"At last!" Angela dropped the wooden fork she's been using to stir a huge vat of *tagliatelle* and rushed towards us, throwing her arms around my neck. She moved to Mario to throw her arms around his neck too, before coming back to me.

"We thought we'd surprise you and cook you a welcome home dinner."

Ercolino had got up from the chair where he had been sitting when we had come in. The creases on his face had almost swallowed up his eyes entirely and his mouth was spread wide in a huge grin that showed his small white teeth.

"I'm so glad you came to your senses before it was too late.

210

Now come and give me a hug. You too, Mario." And although he was smaller than either of us, Ercolino reached out to gather both of us up in a tight embrace.

The kitchen table was laid with a flowered cloth and four places. Ercolino went to the fridge and pulled out a bottle of prosecco.

"I hope you don't mind us letting ourselves in like this." He popped open the bottle and poured a glass for each of us. "We let ourselves in through the back door and then put the keys back on the hook.

"We wanted to show you how happy we are with your news. She's one of the family." Ercolino raised his glass in my direction. Then he raised it again and looked at Mario.

"And that means so are you."

"I'll never get into my wedding dress if I carry on eating like this." I groaned. As well as *tagliatelle* with mushrooms, Angela had cooked escalopes of veal and fried potatoes.

"You women drive me round the wall! Anyway, you've still got plenty of weight to put back on, so eat up and stop moaning."

"So how far have you got with all the preparations?" Angela was sitting opposite me, piling the veal and potatoes onto plates and passing them round.

Our description of the meetings with the two priests drew snorts of disdain from Ercolino who, as a Communist was also a committed anti-cleric.

"What about the reception?"

"We'll do that at the restaurant right next to the abbey itself," said Mario. "We were planning on going up there tomorrow."

"Then there are the invitations to get out, the cake to order and of course my dress to organise. We haven't got much time if it's all going to be ready by the end of August. We've chosen Saturday the 30th as the date."

"If you ask me, Angela, it's a bloody good job you and I decided to elope, instead of going through all this fuss."

Angela kissed Ercolino's cheek fondly.

"What about the *bombonieri*?"

"What on earth are those?"

"They're the little gifts you give each guest as they leave after the reception. It's a kind of memento, and it always contains some sugared almonds, to symbolise the bitter sweet side of marriage."

"You can say that again." Ercolino was sipping a coffee laced with sambuca now, and he winked at me across the table.

"Don't take any notice of him. He still brings me flowers, every time he goes out for a walk. Anyway, let me know if I can help you with anything. I could make the *bombonieri,* if you like."

"Do you remember how funny it was, when Don Gaetano forgot to turn up to conduct the ceremony at our wedding? I wish I'd had a photograph of your look of horror when you drove up to the abbey with Ercolino in his little red car and you realised the priest wasn't there yet. Your face was an absolute picture."

Mario clinked his flute glass of champagne to mine and gently tweaked the miniature toes of the small baby sleeping peacefully next to us.

"I'll never forget it. And then Cesare and Mirella had to dash off to Don Gaetano's house to wake him up from his afternoon siesta. He'd forgotten all about us."

Mario bent down to stroke the baby's few strands of bright blond hair. We were back in the restaurant outside the abbey where we had been married exactly one year earlier.

"Shhhh. Don't wake him up or we'll never be able to eat our dinner and I'm starving." It was a standing joke between us that, since our baby son had arrived two months earlier, we had never been able to sit down to a meal together.

"Starvin' 'ungry, you mean. Anyway, he usually waits till one of us has got a fork in our hand before he wakes up and starts crying. I swear he's got antennae."

"I thought Ercolino was going to punch Don Gaetano on the nose when he finally turned up, nearly one hour late. You know how he hates priests."

"Still, it was a wonderful wedding. Everyone got on so well with each other. The English side and the Italian side. By the end of the evening, you could hardly tell them apart."

Antonio the maître d'hôtel was making his way to our table, taking care to step around the pram and the sleeping baby. Balanced on one hand was a ceramic platter of *strangozzi* with truffles and in the other, a bottle of our favourite *bianco di Decugnano*.

"I've taken the liberty of reproducing exactly the same menu as you had at your wedding reception." He chuckled as he expertly divided the pasta into two bowls and set them in front of us with a flourish. As he had been the first time we had met, when Mario and I had gone to discuss the menu for our reception, Antonio was impeccably dressed in a dark suit and grey silk tie. At the time I had found his stiff formality rather off-putting, and we had nearly fallen out when I had questioned his estimate that we should cater for a quarter of a bottle of wine per head.

"For a six-course dinner? You do realise that half the guests are English? They'll finish a quarter of a bottle with the starters," I had said.

"*Signorina*, I have been doing this job for a great many years, and I can assure you that I have never yet got it wrong," Antonio had replied, somewhat peevishly. "Trust me. A quarter of a bottle will be quite sufficient."

Now Antonio uncorked the bottle of *Decugnano* and sniffed the cork before pouring a small glass for Mario to taste.

"I was just remembering that day a year ago. You had warned me that people would drink a lot of wine, but I didn't quite believe you. Then I saw the whole long table erupt in a Mexican wave." He shook his head at the memory. "I spent the rest of the evening running back and forwards to our cellar to fetch more wine. I've never seen anything quite like it." He shook his head again and drew himself back up to his usual straight-backed position.

"I'll let you get on with your dinner *Signori*. *Buon appetito!*"

I lowered my fork into the glistening pile of pasta and black truffles. A fitful squawking sound came from the pram, first quietly, then becoming louder and louder. Mario bent down to lift the small creature into his arms, jiggling him up and down and cooing softly into his crumpled face. We both knew that this was the end of our romantic dinner for two.

"We'll take it in turns." I shovelled a forkful of pasta into my mouth. There was no time to be lost. Mario tore his gaze away from his now happily gurgling son and picked up his glass.

"Happy anniversary *amore mio*. I don't think we'll forget this one in a hurry."

"Happy anniversary my love. I don't think we ever will."